My Heart Speaks

Wisdom from Pope John XXIII

Jeanne Kun, General Editor

the WORD
among us

The Word Among Us Press
9639 Doctor Perry Road
Ijamsville, Maryland 21754
ISBN: 0-932085-34-2
www.wau.org

Cover design by David Crosson

Made and printed in the United States of America

Library of Congress Cataloging-in-Publication Data

John XXIII, Pope, 1881-1963.
      My heart speaks : wisdom from Pope John XXIII / Jeanne Kun,
general editor.
            p.   cm.
ISBN 0-932085-34-2
  1.   John XXIII, Pope, 1881-1963—Quotations. I. Kun, Jeanne, 1951-
     II. Title

BX1378.2.J6494 A25 2000
282'.092—dc21
[B]
                                            00-035914

Table of Contents

Introduction

When Angelo Giuseppe Roncalli was elected pope on October 28, 1958, he was greeted with joy and enthusiasm by people all over the world. Taking the name John XXIII, he soon became known as the "Good Pope," the "Parish Priest of the World," "Everyone's Pope," or simply "Papa" Giovanni. An Italian peasant in origin and appearance and unpretentious in character, he quickly found his way into the hearts of people of all creeds with his warmth and compassion and by the naturalness he brought to the papacy. Here was a man—sensitive, perceptive, and holy—who translated his faith, charity, and humility into forthright action.

Nearly seventy-seven years old at the beginning of his pontificate, John XXIII was considered by many to be a short-term "compromise" or "transitional" pope, chosen to satisfy both conservative and more progressive elements in the church of the 1950s. He would do little more, some anticipated, than maintain the status quo for a few years' time. Instead, this new pope called for the Second Vatican Council to "open the windows and air out the church." In the four and one-half years of his papacy, he initiated a new age in the church's life and history. As the Jesuit theologian Karl Rahner noted, "The transitional Pope John XXIII effected the transition of the church into the future."

Pope John desired the church to speak to the contemporary world in a language it could understand. While safeguarding the immutable truths of the faith, he encouraged a new formulation of the ancient message of Catholicism: one applicable to the social, political, and technological milieu and concerns of the modern era. His pontificate and the Second Vatican Council set the search for this language and formulation in motion. This process is still being energetically carried out by Pope John Paul II, who has guided the church by the inspirations of the council and seeks to fully and faithfully apply the wisdom and riches of the council's teachings and documents.

John XXIII's pontificate was strongly marked by his efforts to foster unity among Christians and promote *aggiornamento* (renewal in Italian). In an age shadowed by the threat of nuclear destruction and burdened by an unjust distribution of the world's wealth and resources, the pope was a spokesman for peace, mutual cooperation among nations, and social justice.

The selections in this book have been chosen from the vast collection of Angelo Roncalli's writings. For more than sixty years, he kept a spiritual journal of his inner life and an active correspondence with his large family. As bishop and pope, he addressed his brothers in the church's hierarchy, those of other Christian denominations whom he warmly called his "separated brethren," leaders of the nations of the world, faithful Catholics everywhere, and even, in his homilies and encyclicals, nonbelievers. No one was excluded from his wide embrace.

The writings gathered here have been grouped into chapters reflecting the great interests and "love affairs" of Roncalli's heart: his interior life with God, his relationships with his family, peace, unity, truth, and the opening of the Second Vatican Council. The book closes with the highlights of council documents—the fruits of Pope John XXIII's inspiration. A brief biography at the beginning of the book introduces readers to Angelo Roncalli and the events in his life that led to his election as pope.

The editors at *The Word Among Us Press* have taken the liberty of providing titles and subtitles to identify the main thrust of each selection and help the reader through each passage. As you read, you will notice that Pope John XXIII spoke of himself in his encyclicals and public papal speeches in the first-person plural, "we" and "our." We have retained this form, as it reflects the custom and practice of his era. Where the pope used a form of direct address—for example, "venerable brothers"—to his hearers or readers, this has also been left unaltered. In addition, readers will notice the "noninclusive" language that was commonly used at the time.

It is our hope that *My Heart Speaks* will remind us that the vision and hopes of the "Good Pope" are still alive and unfolding in the church and world in this new century. May we take part in this great venture with faith and confidence in the Holy Spirit—that same Spirit whom John XXIII invited to blow with fresh winds over all the earth.

Jeanne Kun
General Editor

Patricia Mitchell
Wisdom Series Editor
The Word Among Us Press

"I Am Your Brother"

THE LIFE OF POPE JOHN XXIII
By Patricia Mitchell

The new pope is . . . like the son of Jacob who, meeting with his brothers, showed them the tenderness of his heart and, bursting into tears, said, "I am Joseph, your brother."

Angelo Giuseppe Roncalli, nearly seventy-seven years old and newly installed as Pope John XXIII, surprised the crowds at St. Peter's Basilica the morning of November 4, 1958, by speaking these words directly to them. It was to be a papacy full of surprises and new beginnings.

Like the Old Testament Joseph, Pope John XXIII reached out to others in the family of Christ and beyond. His warmth, wit, and obvious love for people broke down age-old barriers between nations and churches, and his inspiration for an ecumenical council launched the church on a dramatic journey of brotherhood. "Whenever I see a wall between Christians," he once said, "I try to pull out a brick."

An Unlikely Candidate

If anyone was surprised by his election, it was Roncalli himself. He never wanted to be more than a humble priest like the pastor who mentored him in his own small village. Born in a cold rainstorm on November 25, 1881, in Sotto Il Monte in northern Italy, Angelo was the fourth child and first son of Giovanni and Marianna Roncalli. The family would grow to ten children, joined by a host of relatives, living in poverty as sharecroppers on unforgiving Lombardy soil that barely provided enough food for everyone.

"We were very poor, but so was everyone, so we didn't realize that we lacked anything," Roncalli would say later about his childhood. In the three hundred-year-old farmhouse in which he lived, the cows shared the ground floor with the family, and polenta, a cornmeal dish, was the standard supper fare. Each day opened with Mass, which Angelo often served, and ended with the rosary.

Don Francesco Rebuzzini, the village priest who taught the primary grades at the village school, soon recognized Angelo's potential and helped to guide his studies. He even arranged for him to learn Latin from a parish priest in the neighboring town. It was apparent, both to Don Francesco and to Angelo himself, that he was called to the priesthood. "I do not remember a time when I did not want to be a priest," Roncalli once said. In 1892, when he was eleven years old, Angelo entered the seminary in nearby Bergamo.

Although life at the seminary was rigorous, Angelo was happy. The stocky peasant boy, whose expressive brown eyes would always be his defining feature, was accustomed to the long hours and hard work of farming. In 1895, at the age of fourteen, he began keeping a journal, filled with his private thoughts, prayers, and resolutions. These writings, which he continued throughout his life, were collected and published after his death under the title *Journal of a Soul*.

Learning to Trust

As Roncalli's life unfolded, it became clear that each circumstance he encountered was ordained by God to prepare him for his final mission. Every situation required him to trust that God knew what was better for him than he did himself. In 1900, Roncalli was selected to complete his studies in Rome. This was a great honor, and Roncalli soaked up the history and beauty of the Eternal City. However, the road to ordination was interrupted in 1901, when the Italian government called him into military service.

This difficult year, spent living among the soldiers, was a shock. His sheltered life had not prepared him for the immorality he would witness in the barracks. When the year was over, he wrote in his journal, "I passed through the mire and by [God's] grace I was kept unpolluted." In hindsight, however, he realized that the experience had given him a greater understanding of human weakness and helped him to become a better pastor.

After being ordained in 1904, Roncalli returned to Bergamo, where he was chosen to become secretary to the new bishop. Giacomo Radini Tedeschi—one of Italy's most progressive bishops—had been a leader in the Catholic Action social movement and took controversial stands supporting workers' rights. The bishop's vision of an activist church that treasured its traditions but adapted to the conditions and needs of the time made a strong impression on his new secretary.

When iron workers in nearby Ranica went on strike, Radini Tedeschi's open and generous support of them was highly criticized. In a biography that Roncalli later wrote of the bishop, he said that Radini Tedeschi "resolutely took the side of the striking workers because in doing so he fulfilled a highly Christian duty and acted for justice, charity, and social peace. He let the shouters go on shouting and went calmly on his own way, taking an active part on behalf of the striking workers." Understandably, Roncalli was grief-stricken when his mentor died in 1914.

A Willing Teacher and Reluctant Diplomat

After another stint in the military during Word War I—this time as a chaplain in Bergamo—Roncalli opened a student hostel and taught at the seminary. As the hostel grew in popularity and he became an effective teacher and spiritual director, Roncalli thought he had found his calling. "Now there is no more cause for uncertainty, or for looking for something else; my main task is here, and here is my burden, the apostolate among students." It was where he felt most comfortable, and he seemed to have a pastoral gift.

However, God had other plans—a string of diplomatic posts that exposed him to life beyond Italy and broadened his view of the church and its needs. In 1921, he was appointed to work for the missionary societies, a position that required much overseas travel. Roncalli would have preferred to stay in Bergamo at the students' hostel, the "darling" of his heart. But he had taken for his motto one borrowed from Cardinal Cesare Baronius, the disciple of St. Philip Neri: Obedience and Peace. "These words are in a way my own history and my life," he wrote later.

In 1925, Roncalli was appointed apostolic visitor and the pope's envoy to Bulgaria. He was also consecrated a bishop. Yet, even though he was so far from home, Giuseppe's large family remained his anchor. He spent long holidays with them and sent guidance—and money—when he couldn't visit them in person. More than once, he took on large debts himself to help out family members. His deep desire to remain connected to his family and to everyday people continued to define and nourish him during these challenging years.

In Bulgaria, Roncalli quickly made inroads in Catholic-Orthodox relations. He was awed by Eastern religious art and often turned up unexpectedly at Orthodox monasteries to view their treasures. He seemed to have an innate sense of the common brotherhood between people, regardless of their nationality or religion. His natural tendency was to focus on what united people rather than what divided them.

A Prolonged Mission

As the years in Bulgaria wore on, Roncalli could not help but feel isolated and forgotten. "My prolonged mission . . . often causes me acute and intimate suffering," he wrote in 1933, "but . . . I bear and will bear everything willingly, even joyfully, for the love of Jesus."

Finally, in 1935, at the age of fifty-three, he was sent to Turkey and Greece to become apostolic delegate. At the time, the government in Turkey was hostile to all religions and banned religious dress in public. Determined to protect the Catholic minority in the country, Roncalli complied with the edict, saying: "If in Rome Christ is a Roman, let him be a Turk in Turkey." He also introduced Turkish into the parts of the liturgy that had been traditionally said in French or Italian, including parts of the gospel and his own sermons. This drew some criticism, but did not deter the bishop. "The apostolic vicar is a bishop for everyone and intends honoring the gospel, which does not admit national monopolies," Roncalli said.

Roncalli proved himself adept at politics and diplomacy. Turkey was a neutral country in World War II, and the last way out of Nazi-occupied Europe to Palestine. When thousands of Jews from Slovakia were in Bulgaria and in danger of being sent to concentration camps, Bishop Roncalli intervened and, with the help of the king of Bulgaria, obtained transit visas for them to go to Palestine. In his Pentecost sermon delivered in Istanbul in 1944, Roncalli pointed out that Jesus came to break down the barriers of race, religion, and culture: "He died to proclaim universal brotherhood; the central point of his teaching is charity, that is the love which binds all men to him as the elder brother, and binds us all with him to the Father."

On December 6, 1944, Roncalli received a telegram that shocked him. He had been appointed nuncio to France, an important and sensitive post. He was sixty-three years old. "For the mission now entrusted to me," he wrote to his family, "I would need to be ten years younger. I shall do my best." Even though he was unknown to most of the French, Roncalli's affability and wit quickly won him admiration and respect. As the diplomatic representative of the pope, Roncalli tried to make sure that he did not interfere in the internal problems that faced France. This did not stop him, however, from quietly urging French authorities to release thousands of German prisoners of war who remained incarcerated years after the war had ended.

A Shepherd at Last

Finally, in 1953, at the age of seventy-one, Roncalli was appointed Patriarch of Venice and made a cardinal. It was love at first sight. The Venetians found their new bishop joyful, accessible, and down-to-earth. For his part, Roncalli rejoiced in finally becoming a pastor again. He told them, "Now that I am a shepherd at last, your shepherd, my first desire is to count the sheep, one by one."

The cardinal quickly became a familiar sight in Venice, and could often be seen walking through the squares of the city. While the glories of Venice surrounded him, he also became aware of a pervasive poverty that forced many young people to leave the city in search of jobs. Roncalli appealed to business and community leaders to be "the ministers of providence for all the human family." Inscribed above his door were the words *Pastor et Pater* (Shepherd and Father), a reminder of the kind of bishop he wanted to be. In a diocesan synod in 1957, he stressed the need for bishops to guard against the twin threats of authoritarianism, which "suffocates truth," and paternalism, which "is a caricature of true fatherliness."

Pope Pius XII died on October 9, 1958. After several days of balloting, Cardinal Roncalli emerged as a compromise candidate between those who wanted no change and those who saw the need for the church to keep up with the times. The night before his election, suspecting that he would be made pope, Roncalli was tempted to feel overwhelmed. Instead, he wrote in his diary, "Who is it that rules the church? Is it you or the Holy Ghost? Well, then, Angelo, go to sleep!"

If the cardinals thought this elderly man would be a caretaker pope, they quickly realized that they had misjudged him. When asked what name he had chosen, he surprised everyone by saying, "I will be called John," ending a long succession of Piuses. This break from tradition would be symbolic of the new direction his papacy would take. "The name John is dear to me because it is the name of my father," and because, he added, it was borne by two men who were closest to Christ, John the Baptist and John, the disciple and evangelist. As he prepared to address the crowd in St. Peter's Square, he donned the white pontifical robes, which were too small to fit his portly frame. "I feel trussed up and ready for delivery," he joked to his secretary. He spent his entire first night as pope in prayer.

Anxious not to become a prisoner of the Vatican, Pope John XXIII would sometimes slip out unannounced with his chauffeur. Often his visits were spontaneous. Arriving at a Roman prison the day after Christmas in 1958, he told the inmates, "You could not come to see me so I have come to see you." Even when he walked in the Vatican gardens, Roncalli would chat with the gardeners, asking them about their families and working conditions. When he realized how poorly they were being paid, he ordered a wage increase. Officials in the Vatican curia complained that this would cut into funds allotted for charities, but the pope replied: "The wage increase is a matter of simple justice, and justice comes before charity."

An Inspiration

The idea for a council came to Pope John only three months after his election, on January 20, 1959. "Suddenly," he said, "an inspiration sprang up within me as a flower that blooms in an unexpected springtime." Five days later, he announced his intention to a group of cardinals, who were less than enthusiastic. The idea was revolutionary. Never had a council been called when there was not some issue of doctrine to define or some heresy to combat.

Nevertheless, the work of preparation began. Although no agenda was imposed by Pope John, he made it clear that the purpose of the council was not to change fundamental truths or doctrine, but to present the truth in a more effective way. The pope would continually stress the need for *aggiornamento*, or bringing the church up-to-date. Without this updating, he believed, the church risked being viewed as an archaic and irrelevant institution by an increasingly secularized world. The church had answers to contribute to the problems of the world—answers based on the light and wisdom of the gospel of Jesus Christ.

In another break with tradition—and in the spirit of ecumenism that the pope wanted to bring to the council—Christians from other denominations were invited as observers. Even before the council opened, Pope John received the Archbishop of Canterbury, the head of the Anglican Church. Visits from other church leaders followed.

The week before the council opened, Pope John surprised the world by venturing out of the Vatican to make a pilgrimage to Assisi and Loreto. The trip marked the first time in centuries that a pope had traveled so far from St. Peter's. Upon his return, he closed himself off to spend the next few days in prayer and meditation.

A New Pentecost for the Church

When the council opened on October 11, 1962, Pope John XXIII told the half million people gathered in St. Peter's Square, "Dear children, dear children, I hear your voices!" Pope John watched the first session of the council on closed-circuit television. When it closed in December, he predicted that the second session, scheduled for September 1963, "will be a new Pentecost indeed." The eighty-one-year-old pontiff looked pale and wasted. He was fighting inoperable intestinal cancer, and he knew he would probably not be alive when the council reopened.

Pope John worked on, however. In April 1963, he completed his last encyclical, *Pacem in Terris* (Peace on Earth), a call for respecting the dignity and rights of every human person, and for reason and reconciliation at the height of the Cold War. His desire for peace was put into action during the tense days of the Cuban missile crisis in October 1962, when his public appeals to the United States and the Soviet Union marked the turning point in the resolution of the conflict.

As he lay dying, Pope John whispered over and over the words of Jesus from the Gospel of John (17:11), "May they be one." He died on June 3, 1963—the day after Pentecost. As he predicted, a new Pentecost did descend on the church, renewing it in ways no one could have imagined. The spirit of brotherhood and unity born of the Second Vatican Council, born in the heart of Angelo Giuseppe Roncalli, did not die with him. It has animated the church ever since.

2

"My Soul Is in These Pages"

Angelo Roncalli began keeping a journal in 1895, when he was barely fourteen years old, and continued the practice throughout his lifetime. The final entry was written a few months before his death at the age of eighty-one. Pope John XXIII called these diaries his "journal of a soul," a title suggested to him in his youth and the one that he used as a heading for his notes in 1902.

Journal of a Soul is a unique document, since there is no other known collection of personal and spiritual writings recording the whole life of a priest who became pope. In his journal, Roncalli wrote down his private thoughts, meditations, prayers, and resolutions. Most of these notes were recorded at night by the light of a flickering oil lamp during the various retreats Roncalli made throughout his long life. He kept the bundles of dog-eared pages and rumpled copybooks near at hand and often reread old passages.

Spontaneous and relentlessly honest, Roncalli's notes reflect a constant examination of his life and an ardent desire to fulfill God's will and purpose at each stage of his service to the church. The journal reveals the intimate feelings of a youth eagerly striving to please God and his gradual transformation into a mature, holy, and charitable man. These pages contain the account of Roncalli's profound relationship with God and his growth, year by year, as he resolutely kept in step with the rhythms of nature and grace.

In the spring of 1961, the papal secretary, Don Loris Capovilla, was preparing a collection of the pope's speeches for publication. Capovilla asked Pope John if his private notes might be published as well. "At first I felt some reluctance about publishing and letting others republish my private papers," the pope said later. "I am well aware that people want to know everything about a pope, and everything may be useful to historians. But they are a more intimate part of me than anything else I have written; my soul is in these pages." He agreed that they could be published after his death. "They will do some good to souls who feel drawn towards the priesthood and the more intimate union with God."

JESUS IS CALLING

February 1900, on retreat as a seminarian in Bergamo:

A divine hand has traced for me the path that leads to the altar. Seclusion, prayer and work. To pray, working and to work, praying. To work hard at my studies, always: that is my duty. To study and not boast of my learning, to study untiringly and draw closer to Jesus who is the giver of light, the reflection of eternal light (cf. Wisdom 7:26), and to pray in such a way that study itself may become prayer. In this world there is no getting away from it: we must bend our shoulders to the task. Let us then make a good start and work for love, for this is what the Lord wills. And working with Jesus in Nazareth in prayerful seclusion, I will prepare myself to accomplish more perfectly the mission which awaits me, a mission of wisdom and love, and I shall deserve to be crowned by Jesus with the starry crown of the apostolate.

Here is a thought that might help me. When Jesus was drawing near to the village of Bethany some people ran to tell Mary of his coming, saying: "The Teacher is here and is calling for you!" (John 11:28). What beautiful words! Imagine the loving haste with which Mary ran to greet her divine guest. Well, at the beginning of every one of my actions I will suppose that the bell says: "The Teacher is here and is calling for you." When I reflect that Jesus the Master is here, calling me to study, to pray, to rest, to walk—how can I fail to be at once inspired to do my duties as they should be done, with Jesus instructing me as I do them? ➰

A LIFELINE TO GOD

October 1912, on retreat while serving as secretary to Bishop Giacomo Radini Tedeschi of Bergamo:

I am about to enter the thirty-second year of my life. The thought of the past makes me humble and ashamed; the thought of the present is consoling because mercy is still being shown to me; the thought of the future encourages me in the hope of making up for lost time. How much future will there be? Perhaps a very short one. But long or short as it may be, O Lord, once more I tell you that it is all yours.

I must not try to find or follow new ways of doing good. I live under obedience, and obedience has already overburdened me with so many occupations that my shoulders are sagging under the weight. But I am willing to bear this and other burdens, if the Lord so desires. My rest will be in heaven. These are the years for hard work. My bishop sets me an example, since he does more than I. I will be most careful never to waste a single moment.

I find it humiliating, but it is my duty to insist again on the resolutions already made about being absolutely faithful to my rule of life. Getting up at half past five, then meditation, the bishop's Mass, my Mass, thanksgiving, the Hours; brief but frequent visits to the Blessed Sacrament, Vespers after my brief siesta, a very devout recital of the rosary; after supper Matins and Lauds, without fail, and a rather longer visit to the Blessed Sacrament; some spiritual reading before falling asleep. These are the fundamental points: they are my lifeline.

O Lord, I acknowledge my weakness; help me to keep strictly to these practices. Help me so that next year I shall not need shamefacedly to confess once more my infidelity. ❧

WITHOUT A BACKWARD GLANCE

January 1924, on retreat in Rome while in the service of the Propagation of the Faith:

Today, 18 January, the Feast of St. Peter's Chair, it is three years since I began, under obedience, my work as President for Italy of the Propagation of the Faith in the World. You have always been with me, O Lord Jesus, and good and merciful: "Thy decrees are very sure" (Psalm 93:5). To my sorrow, I left behind in Bergamo what I loved so much: the seminary, where the bishop had appointed my most unworthy self as spiritual director, and the students' hostel, the darling of my heart. I have thrown myself, heart and soul, into my new work. Here I must and will stay, without a thought, a glance or a desire for anything else, especially as the Lord gives me indescribable happiness here.

Anyone who judges me from appearances takes me for a calm and steady worker. It is true that I work; but deep in my nature there is a tendency towards laziness and distraction. This tendency must, with the help of God, be forcibly resisted. To humble myself constantly I will always tell myself that I am a lazy fellow, a beast of burden that ought to do much more work and get on with it much faster, and so deserves to be beaten. I must be particularly careful not to procrastinate but to do at once what is most urgent. In everything, however, I must keep and impart to others that calm and composure with which alone things can be done and done properly. I will not worry if others are in a hurry. He who is always in a hurry, even in the business of the church, never gets very far. ❧

OBEDIENCE AND PEACE

*March 1925, on retreat in Rome in preparation
for his consecration as a bishop:*

I have not sought or desired this new ministry: the Lord has chosen me, making it clear that it is his will that it would be a grave sin for me to refuse. So it will be for him to cover up my failings and supply my insufficiencies. This comforts me and gives me tranquility and confidence. . . .

The church is making me a bishop in order to send me to Bulgaria, to fulfill there, as apostolic visitor, a mission of peace. Perhaps I shall find many difficulties awaiting me. With the Lord's help, I feel ready for everything. I do not seek, I do not desire, the glory of this world; I look forward to greater glory in heaven.

Now, forever, I assume also the name of Joseph, one of the names given me at my baptism, in honor of the dear Patriarch who will always be my chief protector, after Jesus and Mary, and my model. My other special protectors will be St. Francis Xavier, St. Charles, St. Francis de Sales, the patron saints of Rome and Bergamo, and the Blessed Gregory Barbarigo.

I insert in my coat of arms the words *Obœdientia et Pax* (Obedience and Peace) which Cesare Baronius used to say every day, when he kissed the Apostle's foot [a statue] in St. Peter's. These words are in a way my own history and my life. O may they be the glorification of my humble name through the centuries! ❧

TOTAL ABANDONMENT TO GOD'S WILL

December 1928, on retreat on the Bosporus while serving as apostolic visitor in Bulgaria:

Twenty-five years a priest! I think of all the ordinary and special graces I have received, of my preservation from grave sins, innumerable opportunities of doing good, sound bodily health, undisturbed tranquility of mind, good reputation among men, immensely superior to my deserts, and the successful outcome of the various undertakings entrusted to me under obedience. . . .

In twenty-five years of priesthood what innumerable failings and deficiencies! My spiritual organism still feels healthy and robust, thanks to God, but what weaknesses! . . .

Therefore I must always see myself as the poor wretch that I am, the least and most unworthy of the bishops of the church, barely tolerated among my brethren out of pity and compassion, deserving none but the lowest place: truly the servant of all, not merely in words but in a profound inner sense and outward appearance of humility and submission.

During this spiritual retreat I have felt once more,

and most keenly, that it is my duty to be truly holy. The Lord does not promise me twenty-five years of episcopal life, but he does tell me that if I wish to become holy, he gives me the time I need and the necessary graces.

Jesus, I thank you, and I promise you, heaven and earth being my witnesses, that I will make every effort to succeed, beginning from now. Most holy Mary, my kind heavenly Mother, St. Joseph, my dearest protector, I call upon you to be my sureties for the promise I make this day before the throne of Jesus, and I implore you to succor me, help me, that I may be faithful.

It is not difficult for me now to understand that the beginning of sanctity lies in my total abandonment to the Lord's holy will, even in little things, and that is why I must insist on this. I do not wish or ask for anything beyond obedience to the dispositions, instructions and wishes of the Holy Father and the Holy See.

I will never take any step, direct or indirect, to bring any change or alteration in my situation, but I will in all things and at all times live from day to day, letting others say and do, and suffering whoever so desires to pass ahead of me, without preoccupying myself about my future. ❧

ENTRUSTED TO GOD'S MERCY

*April 1945, on retreat during Holy Week
while serving as papal nuncio in France:*

H*e that trusteth in God shall never fare the worse* (cf. Ecclesiastes 32:28). The events of my life during the last three months are a constant source of amazement and confusion to me. I have had to renew very frequently my good resolution not to preoccupy myself with my future or try to obtain anything for myself!

Here I am now, transported from Istanbul to Paris, with the initial difficulties of introduction overcome, I hope successfully. Once again my motto *Obœdientia et Pax* has brought a blessing. All this is a good reason for mortifying myself and seeking a more profound humility and trustful confidence, in order to consecrate to the Lord, for the sanctification of my own soul and the edification of others, the years I still have to live and serve Holy Church.

I must not disguise from myself the truth: I am definitely approaching old age. My mind resents this and almost rebels, for I still feel so young, eager, agile and alert. But one look in my mirror disillusions me. This is the season of maturity; I must do more and better, reflecting that perhaps the time still granted to me for living is brief, and that I am drawing near to the gates of eternity. This thought caused Hezekiah to turn to the wall and weep (cf. 2 Kings 20:2). I do not weep.

No, I do not weep, and I do not even desire to live my life over again, so as to do better. I entrust to the Lord's mercy whatever I have done, badly or less than well, and I look to the future, brief or long as it may be here below, because I want to make it holy and a source of holiness to others. ❧

SHEPHERD AND PASTOR OF SOULS

*May 1953, on retreat while
cardinal patriarch of Venice:*

It is interesting to note that Providence has brought me back to where I began to exercise my priestly vocation, that is to pastoral work. Now I am ministering directly to souls. To tell the truth, I have always believed that, for an ecclesiastic, diplomacy (so-called!) must be imbued with the pastoral spirit; otherwise it is of no use and makes a sacred mission look ridiculous. Now I am confronted with the church's real interests, relating to her final purpose, which is to save souls and guide them to heaven. This is enough for me and I thank the Lord for it. I said so in St. Mark's in Venice on 15 March, the day of my solemn entry. I desire and think of nothing else but to live and die for the souls entrusted to me. "The good shepherd gives his life for his sheep . . . I am come that they may have life, and may have it more abundantly" (John 10:11 and 10).

I am beginning my direct ministry at an age—seventy-two years—when others end theirs. So, *I find myself on the threshold of eternity.* O Jesus, Chief Shepherd and Bishop of our souls, the mystery of my life and death is in your hands, close to your heart. On the one hand I tremble at the approach of my last hour; on the other hand I trust in you and only look one day ahead. I feel I am in the same condition as St. Aloysius Gonzaga, that is, I must go on with what I have to do, always striving after perfection but thinking still more of God's mercy.

In the few years I have still to live, *I want to be a holy pastor,* in the full sense of the word, like the Blessed Pius X, my predecessor, and the revered Cardinal Ferrari, and my own Mgr. Radini Tedeschi while he lived, and as he would have remained had he lived longer. "So help me God." ❧

LORD, BE MY STRENGTH

December 1959, on retreat in the Vatican at the end of his first year as pope:

Since the Lord chose me, unworthy as I am, for this great service, I feel I have no longer any special ties in this life, no family, no earthly country or nation, nor any particular preferences with regard to studies or projects, even good ones. Now, more than ever, I see myself only as the humble and unworthy "servant of God and servant of the servants of God." The whole world is my family. This sense of belonging to everyone must give character and vigor to my mind, my heart and my actions.

This vision, this feeling of belonging to the whole world, will give a new impulse to my constant and continual daily prayer: the Breviary, Holy Mass, the whole rosary and my faithful visits to Jesus in the tabernacle, all varied and ritual forms of close and trustful union with Jesus.

The experience of this first year gives me light and strength in my efforts to straighten, to reform, and tactfully and patiently to make improvements in everything.

Above all, I am grateful to the Lord for the temperament he has given me, which preserves me from anxieties and tiresome perplexities. I feel I am under obedience in all things and I have noticed that this disposition, in great things and in small, gives me, unworthy as I am, a strength of daring simplicity, so wholly evangelical in its nature that it demands and obtains universal respect and edifies many. "Lord, I am not worthy. O Lord, be always my strength and the joy of my heart. My God, my mercy." ❧

READY FOR LIFE OR DEATH

*August 10, 1961, on retreat at Castel Gandolfo,
the summer papal residence:*

When on 28 October, 1958, the cardinals of the Holy Roman Church chose me to assume the supreme responsibility of ruling the universal flock of Jesus Christ, at seventy-seven years of age, everyone was convinced that I would be a provisional and transitional pope. Yet here I am, already on the eve of the fourth year of my pontificate, with an immense program of work in front of me to be carried out before the eyes of the whole world, which is watching and waiting. As for myself, I feel like St. Martin, who "neither feared to die, nor refused to live."

I must always hold myself ready to die, even a sudden death, and also to live as long as it pleases the Lord to leave me here below. Yes, always. At the beginning of my eightieth year I must hold myself ready: for death or life, for the one as for the other, and I must see to the saving of my soul. Everyone calls me "Holy Father," and holy I must and will be. ❧

HEARTS BEATING TOGETHER

*August 14, 1961, on the same
retreat at Castel Gandolfo:*

Considering the purpose of my own life I must:

(1)   Desire only to be virtuous and holy, and so
be pleasing to God.
(2)   Direct all things, thoughts as well as
actions, to the increase, the service and the
glory of Holy Church.
(3)   Recognize that I have been set here by
God, and therefore remain perfectly serene
about all that happens, not only as regards
myself but also with regard to the church,
continuing to work and suffer with Christ,
for her good.
(4)   Entrust myself at all times to Divine
Providence.
(5)   Always acknowledge my own nothingness.
(6)   Always arrange my day in an intelligent
and orderly manner.

My life as a priest, or rather—as I am called to my
honor and shame—as Prince of the whole priesthood
of Christ, in his name and by his power, unfolds
before the eyes of my divine Master, the great
Lawgiver. He looks down on me as he hangs on the

Cross, his body torn and stained with blood. His side is wounded, his hands and feet are pierced. He looks at me and invites me to gaze on him. Justice led him straight to love, and love immolated him. This must be my lot: "The disciple is not above his master" (Matthew 10:24).

O Jesus, here I am before you. You are suffering and dying for me, old as I am now and drawing near the end of my service and my life. Hold me closely, and near to your heart, letting mine beat with yours.

3

"To My Beloved Family"

Angelo Roncalli kept up an active correspondence with his large, close-knit family. His earliest letters were written from Rome during his days there as a seminarian, and the last were written from his papal office in the Vatican.

Roncalli wrote as a son, grandson, nephew, brother, uncle, friend—and ever a priest—to his wide circle of family members. His letters spanned six decades, from 1901 to 1962, years marked by two world wars, a long succession of popes and kings, and extraordinary technological advances as well as by changes and advances in his service to the church. The letters trace the development of his priestly vocation and his relentless efforts to follow God's will.

Roncalli's letters also reveal the story of his human relationships. Writing to simple people of peasant stock in words full of warmth and affection, Roncalli offered strength and spiritual guidance to four generations of his immediate and extended family. Unfailingly kind and loving yet always frank and direct, he bolstered the faith of his grandfather and uncle, his parents, his brothers and sisters and their spouses, and his nieces and nephews. His aim was to cultivate love, harmony, and obedience to God's will in their lives and homes.

When Pope John reread the collection of letters late in his life, he did not change or repudiate anything he had written in earlier years. Rather, he remarked, "You will not find here a disrespectful word about anyone, or an expression which I now regret." These letters, more than seven hundred of them, were published a few years after Pope John XXIII's death in a collection entitled *Letters to His Family*. ෴

MAY YOU ALL BE GOOD CHRISTIANS

† Jesus, Mary, Joseph
Rome, 16 February 1901

My beloved parents, brothers, sisters, grandfather and uncle,

When you read this letter of mine you will all have benefited spiritually from this Mission you are attending, which will soon be over. I rejoice with you and from my heart congratulate you on having this fine and enviable opportunity of once more devoting some serious thought to the salvation of your souls and to your eternal happiness in Paradise.

This is what I most desire for you, for I have never wished or implored from heaven for my family the good things of this world—wealth, pleasures, success—

but rather that you should all be good Christians, virtuous and resigned in the loving arms of Divine Providence, and living at peace with everyone.

In fact what use would it be for us to possess even all the gold in the world at the price of losing our souls? Keep this truth firmly fixed in your minds and never forget it.

We must never feel saddened by the very straitened circumstances in which we live; we must be patient, look above and think of Paradise.

Paradise, Paradise! We shall find our rest there, do you understand? There we shall suffer no more; we shall receive the reward of our works and of our sufferings, if we have borne them with patience.

Direct all your actions and your sacrifices to this end: that they may all serve to make you more happy and content in Paradise.

Think of what the good Jesus did and suffered for us. He endured great poverty, he worked from morning to night, was slandered, persecuted and ill-treated in every way and crucified by the very people whom he loved so much.

We must learn from him not to complain, not to get angry, and not to lose our tempers with anyone, and not to nurse in our hearts any dislike for those we believe have injured us, but to have compassion for one another, because we all have our faults, some of one kind, some of another, and we must love everyone. You understand what I mean? Everyone, even those who injure, or have injured us; we must forgive, and pray for these too. Perhaps in God's eyes they are better than we are.

This is the real lesson you should learn from the

Mission, and this is the only way to live happily, even in this world, even in the midst of so many hardships. And then you must pray, pray always and pray well, and go frequently to confession and to holy communion and have a great love for the Sacred Heart of Jesus and for Our Lady. Hear Holy Mass every day, never miss the homily and the explanation of doctrine. . . .

The Lord wants me to be a priest: that is why he has lavished so many gifts upon me, even sending me here to Rome, to be near his vicar, the pope, in the Holy City, near the tombs of so many illustrious martyrs and so many holy priests. This is a great good fortune for me and for you, for which you must always thank the good God.

But I am not going to be a priest just to please someone else, or to make money, or to find comfort, honors or pleasures. God forbid! It is simply because I want to be able later on to be of some service to poor people, in whatever way I can. And that is why I would like you to be the first to benefit from this, you who have done so much for me, you whose spiritual welfare is so dear to my heart and for whom I pray every day, I might say every hour. . . .

Please remember me, all of you, at the general communion. Meanwhile accept my wishes and my greetings, and share these with all our relations and friends.

Your
Seminarist Angelo

My health is flourishing. Greetings to the reverend parish priest and curate.

CHRISTMAS GREETINGS

Sofia
20 December 1927

My dear parents,

I send to you and all the family, including all my sisters, my best wishes for Christmas. Christmas is the family feast, and always greatest and happiest where there are children, as in our home.

I shall pass the festival peacefully here. But this year I shall sing the solemn Mass in the church of the Catholics of the Latin rite and shall stay to dine with the good friars. As you can imagine, during my three Masses I shall be remembering you all, and praying to the Holy Child for the needs of every one of you, imploring for all, as I always do, the grace that, as we love one another so much on earth, so we may find one another again in Paradise, with not one of us missing. Oh! that would be too dreadful!

My health is very good. I am thinner, but not too thin. Here it is cold but I am able to look after myself well. Yesterday for the second time the snow fell very thickly, and so this morning the cold is more intense. Take proper care of yourselves: this weather is particularly harmful for old people.

To remind you of me on Christmas Day I am sending you the last one hundred lire note I brought back with me from Italy. It is, so to speak, the last cartridge in my belt, and it is a pity there are no more. But this year I shot rather too many, and now I must be a bit more economical. But there is nothing to be afraid of. I am a son of Providence, who will not allow either me or you to go without what we need, and will give us also in due time what is right and proper. This small sum I am sending you is for your Christmas dinner, nothing else.

On that day you will all be together at the Colombera in good and holy company. I shall be with you in the spirit, all smiles and blessings....

May the Lord grant you all his blessings and consolations!

I beg the sisters to take a special blessing from me to the Sisters of the orphanage and to the mother, sister, and uncle of the reverend parish priest.

A kiss, a caress and a special blessing to the children.

Your loving
✝ Angelo Giuseppe
Archbishop

I Mourn With You

After hearing of his father's death:

Constantinople
29 July 1935, evening

My dear mother, brothers and sisters,

So the Lord has wished our sacrifice to be complete. As I said in my telegram this morning, I mourn with you all. Today, as soon as I received the sad telegram, I had to go alone into my chapel and weep like a child. Now I am feeling a little calmer, but my tears are still ready to flow. I console myself by gazing at our dear father's face. His eyes are full of light and happiness. They look at me and at you, from the heaven he has at last entered, as we must hope, through the mercy of the Lord in whom he believed and whom he always loved. How precious now is the memory of his fidelity to his religious duties, to his daily Mass, the lively interest he took in everything connected with the church, his scrupulous honesty and certain charming ways he had of showing his devotion to Mary Immaculate and to the Child Jesus, a devotion which was his lifelong joy and an example to his children and grandchildren.

Although he died at the age of eighty-one I feel as if he was still too young to die. Indeed he was too young for us to lose him; we would have liked him to live for ever, or at least for some years longer. What a welcome Angelino will have given him in Paradise, and our dear sister Enrica, and all the old folks of his family and of our mother's! We must console ourselves by thinking of all these things which are sacred truths: thinking of the heaven where we shall go, where we shall find him again and together enjoy for evermore the holy light and love of God.

You know that one of the greatest consolations of my life is my family, which I am always praising to everyone: poor, simple, humble but good and godfearing. I am sure that, especially on such painful occasions as the deaths of our dearest ones, you will continue to do yourselves honor, with your faith in God, your veneration for our beloved dead, and the dignity and decorum with which you behave even in times of the greatest suffering.

I would like to think that you especially, our beloved mother, find consolation in my words, you who now become even more revered and sacred. But what else can I say? The law of sorrow is the law of nature. Our dear father has become invisible to our eyes, but he still lives with us. He loves us, protects us and awaits us in heaven. Your children gather around you to comfort and support you. Do not tire yourself out looking after them: rest a little. My house at Camaitino is entirely at your disposal. Go there with my sisters. They are so glad to have your company, to look after you and console you: let the others come to see you there. You know that your son the bishop is not rich, but he would sell even his cross to satisfy your desires or your needs. I hope to be with you myself in September. We shall be glad of each other's company. Your Battista has left us at the age of eighty-one; you may think of leaving us when you are ninety, and you will always be the object of our joy and love. . . .

I bless you all together with great and tender affection.

✝ a. g. r.

So Great a Burden

Constantinople
7 December 1944

My dear sisters, brothers and all the family,

Yesterday evening I also received from the Vatican a telegram informing me that the Holy Father is sending me to Paris as apostolic nuncio. I could not believe my eyes, so far was I from imagining so great an honor and so onerous a responsibility. Now we are waiting for the French government to give its *beneplacito*: I ought to leave almost at once, in order to be in Paris for New Year's Day. I cannot describe my feelings: a great distrust and fear of my own capacity to bear so great a burden, and at the same time an even greater confidence in the Lord who is bound to help me because I can safely assert, before God and man, that I have never either desired or sought this post. That out of so many experienced, learned and holy prelates the Holy Father should have sought me out here, where moreover I was so happy and would have been content to stay longer, is certainly characteristic of the ways of Providence that makes use of the humblest creatures, just because they have no pretensions, to further his glorious purposes. How much more now I need to sanctify myself, and how much more too I need your simple prayers! It may indeed be that Paris will be my Calvary, and that a poor man like me is just what is needed to be totally sacrificed in the service of the Holy See in times like these when the restoration of religion is so uncertain and difficult.

I cannot tell you how sad I feel at having to part with these sons and brothers of mine here in Constantinople, where for ten full years I have been father and shepherd. In Paris there will be for me no pastoral ministry, which I enjoy so much and for which I was ordained priest. I shall be almost entirely taken up with religious questions in which politics are frequently involved, and this is always unpleasant. I tell you this to show that I am not moving to Paris for any other purpose than for work and self-sacrifice. For the mission entrusted to me I would need to be ten years younger. I shall do my best as long as my health lasts. . . .

From Paris, if I really go there, I shall write to you at once. My greetings to the reverend parish priest, to whom I shall write. And I bless also the good Sisters at the orphanage, with the children and all who ask news of me.

† a.g.r.

Take Everything Humbly

Paris
30 November 1952

My dear sisters, brothers, nephews,
nieces and relations,

As you see, some news spreads so quickly that the people it most concerns have no time to impart it themselves. So it is true: my humble name is included among the twenty-four churchmen whom the Holy Father, on 12 January, will nominate cardinals of Holy Church. I am sure that you will be pleased to hear this: I too am pleased, more for your sakes than for my own.

Take everything simply and humbly, as I do. Even becoming a cardinal counts for nothing unless it leads to eternal salvation and sanctification. . . .

I admit that this nomination gives me great joy when I think of you, humble Christian people as you are, and of our little native village, and of all who bear our name and are our kith and kin. In these times to have a cardinal in the family does not indicate wealth. I foresee that my material condition will be as before. I shall not lack what I need, but my family will still be living modestly. I too shall always be poor, but poor with honor and dignity. We shall speak of this again. Meanwhile, thank the Lord with me and ask him to make me a good cardinal, a peace-loving and gentle cardinal, working only for Holy

Church and the souls of men. And do not worry about anything. . . .

Here at the Nunciature everyone is rejoicing: Mgr. Testa, etc., etc., the Sisters, the domestic staff—but, as with all earthly things, their joy is mingled with sadness at the thought of the inevitable parting.

That is why it is important above all to keep closely united in prayer to the Lord, who never forsakes his own.

> Your loving
> † Ang. Gius.
> Archbishop

DESIRE NOTHING BUT GOD'S WILL

> Venice
> 8 January 1955

My dear Maria,

The news I receive about your health shows me that it is not improving, and this distresses me greatly. My dear sister Maria, I had thought to pass my last years with you, even if not always together, at least in each other's company much of the time at Camaitino and here in Venice, since our dear Ancilla has left us for Paradise. But now you too fall ill with the same ailment that the Holy Father is suffering from. Every now and then he seems on the point of death and then he recovers, but only to have another relapse. I have very little hope that the Holy Father will get better, in spite of so many doctors and medicines and so many costly cures. His life is a miracle, but miracles, as you know, do not last long. And perhaps we are all wrong, my dear Maria, to complain. When we reach our age every year is extra.

You too are over seventy and as you have never been very strong and are now seriously ill you can only bow your head and say: You have given me seventy years of life, O Lord, and I thank you. If you grant me a longer time I accept it willingly; but your will be done, O Lord, and not my own, on earth as in heaven. This is what our Ancilla used to say and now she is happier than we are. And this is what I say too, Maria. During the Spiritual Exercises this year I was busy drawing up my Will concerning a few things I shall leave behind at Sotto il Monte. My health is good: a little rheumatism every now and then, but on the whole I bear up very well and do everything with great calm. Here I am the most energetic of all the older clerics, and our good people look at me with admiration. In France there are quite a few people who secretly prophesy even greater things for me; some crazy Frenchmen, who rejoice in revelations and second sight, have even announced the name I shall assume when they make me pope. Crazy, crazy, the whole lot of them! I am preparing for my death. I have a fine program of work here for this year and also for the next year when we shall celebrate the fifth centenary of St. Lorenzo Guistiniani, the first Patriarch of Venice. But I keep myself ready and prepared for death every day, and for a good death, desiring nothing else but the Lord's will. You know, Maria, living in this way, every day being ready and prepared for a good death, ends by filling my heart with a profound and serene sense of peace, even greater than I had before, surely a foretaste of heaven where our dear ones are awaiting us.

I know that it is easy to say and to write these things when one is free from bodily pain, and I too sometimes fear my resistance to pain. But with this fear in my heart and the thought of your sufferings, my dear Maria, I still repeat *Thy will be done*, adding the prayer: O Lord, O Blessed Mary, I am weak; give me the strength to bear this pain as a sign of my love for you who were crucified for me....

I shall pray especially for you, Maria, and for all our family, living and dead. The dead watch over us from heaven and give us courage. The living enjoy the Lord's grace while they make their sacrifices for him. I bless you all. Mgr. Loris joins me in prayers and good wishes for you.

> Your loving brother,
> † Angelo Giuseppe
> Cardinal

From My Loving Heart

This letter was published on June 8, 1963, a few days after Pope John XXIII's death:

Vatican
3 December 1961

My dear brother Severo,

I think it is now three years since I last used a type-writer. I used to enjoy typing so much and if today I have decided to begin again, using a machine that is new and all my own, it is in order to tell you that I know that I am growing old—how can I help knowing it with all the fuss that has been made about my eightieth birthday?—but I am still fit, and I continue on my way, still in good health, even if some slight disturbance makes me aware that to be eighty is not the same as being sixty, or fifty. For the present at least I can continue in the service of the Lord and Holy Church.

This letter which I was determined to write to you, my dear Severo, contains a message for all, for Alfredo, Giuseppino, Assunta, our sister-in-law Caterina, your own dear Maria, Virginio and Angelo Ghisleni, and all the members of our large family, and I want it to be to all of them a message from my loving heart, still warm and youthful. Busied as I am, as you all know, in such an important office with the eyes of the whole world upon me, I cannot forget the members of my dear family, to whom my thoughts turn day by day. . . .

My own personal serenity, which makes such an impression on people, derives from this: the obedience in which I have always lived, so that I do not desire or beg to live longer, even a day beyond that hour in which the Angel of Death will come to call me and take me, as I trust, to Paradise.

This does not prevent me from thanking the Lord for having deigned to choose from Brusicco and the Colombera the man who was called to be the direct successor of the popes of twenty centuries and to assume the title of Vicar of Jesus Christ on earth.

Because of this choice the name Roncalli has become known, loved and respected all over the world. You are very wise to keep yourselves very humble, as I try to do, and not let yourselves be influenced by the insinuations and tittle-tattle of the world. All the world wants is to make money, enjoy life, and impose its own will at all costs, even with violence, if this should unhappily seem necessary.

My eighty years of life completed tell me, as they tell you, dear Severo, and all the members of our family, that what is most important is always to keep ourselves well prepared for a sudden departure, because this is what matters most: to make sure of eternal life, trusting in the goodness of the Lord who sees all and makes provision for all. . . .

Go on loving one another, all you Roncallis, with the new families growing up among you, and try to understand that I cannot write to all separately. Our

Giuseppino was right when he said to his brother the pope: "Here you are a prisoner *de luxe*: you cannot do all you would like to do" . . .

I am well aware that you have to bear certain mortifications from people who like to talk nonsense. To have a pope in the family, a pope regarded with respect by the whole world, who yet permits his relations to go on living so modestly, in the same social conditions as before! But many know that the pope, the son of humble but respected parents, never forgets anyone; he has, and shows, a great affection for his nearest kin; moreover, his own condition is the same as that of most of his recent predecessors; and a pope does not honor himself by enriching his relations but only by affectionately coming to their aid, according to their needs and the conditions of each one.

This is and will be one of the finest and most admired merits of Pope John and his Roncallis.

At my death I shall not lack the praise which did so much honor to the saintly Pius X: "He was born poor and died poor." As I have now completed my eighty years, naturally all the others will be coming along after me. Be of good heart! We are in good company. I always keep by my bedside the photograph that gathers all our dead together with their names inscribed on the marble: grandfather Angelo, *barba* Zaverio, our revered parents, our brother Giovanni, our sisters Teresa, Ancilla, Maria and Enrica. Oh what a fine chorus of souls to await us and pray for us! I think of them constantly. To remember them in prayer gives me courage and joy, in the confident hope of joining them all again in the everlasting glory of heaven.

I bless you all, remembering with you all the brides who have come to rejoice the Roncalli family and those who have left us to increase the happiness of new families, of different names but similar ways of thinking. Oh the children, the children, what a wealth of children and what a blessing!

JOANNES XXIII P.p.

4

"That They May Be One"

Angelo Roncalli's understanding and warmth toward all people, and his respect for their dignity, characterized his life as priest, bishop, and pope. He was accessible to everyone, and he constantly tried to soften discord with humility and charity, virtues that made his diplomacy so effective. Consequently, his efforts to promote unity and brotherhood among all nationalities, races, cultures, and denominations were far-reaching, even before he was elected to the papacy.

As papal representative in Bulgaria, Turkey, and Greece, Roncalli stretched out a hand of friendship to those who were Eastern Orthodox. His great sensitivity and discretion resulted in an improved relationship with the Orthodox Church there. "I want to study Turkish with more care and perseverance. I am fond of the Turks, to whom the Lord has sent me," he noted in his journal. "I know that my way of dealing with them is right; above all, it is Catholic and apostolic. I must continue with faith, prudence and sincere zeal, at the cost of any sacrifice." While nuncio in France, he was appointed as the first permanent observer of the Holy See at the United Nations Educational, Scientific and Cultural Organization (UNESCO), where he twice addressed its general assemblies.

As pope, John XXIII broadened the College of Cardinals culturally and internationally, naming the first Indian and African cardinals. He made notable advances in ecumenical relations by creating a new Secretariat for Promoting Christian Unity and by appointing a representative to the Assembly of the World Council of Churches held in New Delhi in 1961. He also welcomed the heads of many churches to the Vatican.

Never before had the presiding bishop of the Protestant Episcopal Church of the United States met with a pope. Not since the fourteenth century had an archbishop of Canterbury set foot inside the Vatican when Archbishop Geoffrey Fisher visited Pope John XXIII in 1960. Lovingly he reminded Christians from other denominations of the words of St. Augustine: "Whether they wish it or not, they are our brethren. They cease to be our brethren only when they stop saying 'Our Father.'"

John XXIII's papacy heralded a new era between Christian churches that had been separated by centuries of painful disagreement and division. The Patriarch Athenagoras of Istanbul said of him, "The pope of Rome is the first leader of Roman Catholicism who has grasped the mystery of Christ's seamless robe, fingered intuitively its warp and woof and its seamless wondrousness."

When once asked about the possibility of the reunion of all Christians, Pope John replied, "I realize that it will take a long time. Neither you nor I will be there to celebrate the great feast of reconciliation. Neither will my immediate successors. But someone must begin to clear away the obstacles that stand in the way of the glorious awakening. At any rate, an attempt should be made. If you want to smooth down rough edges, you must first use a plane." ❧

SOFTENING DISCORD WITH LOVE AND HUMILITY

From an address given as cardinal patriarch of Venice:

Unhappily, during the centuries the seamless robe of Christ has been torn, and it is still rent. Heresies and schisms abound, and in more recent times we see the erection of this dismal Tower of Babel—the great Babylon—a continual affront to our eyes and bitterness to our hearts, this movement called secularization, which means a gradual separation of the ordinary business of life from the whole activity of the church.

This thought grieves every honest mind that is receptive to the grace of the gospel, the love of Christ and of his Holy Church.

Listen to what the aged Cardinal Bessarion said in the fifteenth century: "What excuses can we offer to God for being separated from our brothers when he himself, in order to unite us and gather us into a single fold, came down from heaven, took on our human flesh and was crucified? What will be our defense in the sight of future generations? Let us not have to suffer this shame, venerable Fathers and brothers" (he was speaking to the Fathers of the Council of Florence), "let us not behave in such a manner, or make such poor provision for ourselves and our descendants…"

We are still faced with a most disheartening state of affairs, that we need not describe to you here.

Is the entire responsibility for this to be laid on the shoulders of our separated brothers? It is partly theirs, and in great part our own. . . .

It is our duty to soften the discord with our behavior and our speech, with the example of our humility and charity—with these two virtues above all, for they overcome all resistance. ☙

A BRILLIANT RAINBOW

As papal nuncio, Roncalli presided at Pontifical Vespers in the Church of Saint Joseph des Carmes, Paris, where the Week of Prayer for Christian Unity was being observed. There he gave his first address in France on January 21, 1945.

I am glad that these first words that I say in Paris before an altar are the continuation of those which I last said in Constantinople, today known as Istanbul: an appeal for unity and an expression of our longing for peace.

These shining points, which stand for two worlds and two forms of civilization, Constantinople and Paris, are spanned, as it were, by a brilliant rainbow, upon which glow the last words of the prayer of Jesus, who was about to leave his disciples and wished to comfort them: "That they may be one" (John 17:21).

We have come to pray for Christian Unity and we pray as Catholics; but in order to attain this particular aim we pray in union with our brothers who belong to other Christian confessions: Orthodox, Greek and Slav; Protestants of all shades, peoples of all nationalities and all languages who believe in Christ. . . .

Obedience and Peace

When I was a young professor of history I was interested in that great personage who has rightly been hailed the father of ecclesiastical history, Cardinal Cesare Baronius. I was reading one day what his secretary, Aringhi, wrote about him. . . .

Father Cesare Baronius . . . belonged to the Congregation of the Oratory, and he used to go every day towards evening to the "Chiesa Nuova" near St. Peter's. The little beggar boys who were waiting around the doors of the church, Aringhi tells us, rejoiced as soon as they saw him in the far distance and used to say: "Here comes the priest with the big shoes," alluding to the thick shoes he used to wear. When the priest came up to them he gave a small coin to every one of those urchins, who fell on their knees around him; then he reverently entered the basilica.

Inside he would go straight to the bronze statue of St. Peter, which was then near the door, and kiss the apostle's foot, always pronouncing these two words: *Pax et Obœdientia.* In this brief and simple gesture, so constantly repeated, the whole man comes to life for us. Such words have a profound meaning and, if I mistake not, explain and interpret his whole life. *Pax et Obœdientia.* Peace for his own soul, peace for his brethren, for the church troubled with heresy and for the whole of human society, was the dream and ideal which always cheered him in his unending labors and in the transports of his soul. Obedience of the humblest and blindest sort, a childlike obedience to his father Philip Neri as long as he lived, and obedience to the pope, whoever he was and whatever his character—and in his epoch there was in the Chair of Peter a succession of men, attitudes and ambitions of the most varied kinds—that was his only rule of conduct and, I would add, the real secret of his success.

My very dear brothers, I have said all. I have revealed to you the little secret of my episcopal motto, which I hold very dear, and which has kept me such good company for twenty years.

In this hour of uplifting and encouraging prayer, a prayer which answers the supreme appeal of Jesus "that they may be one," I wish to ask you to seek your peace and inspiration in the *Obœdientia et Pax* of Baronius. He who remains faithful to the spirit which inspires the apostolic activity of the church, strengthened by a joyful obedience and a firm peace of mind, possesses the gift of ensuring domestic and civic order. It is in this order that we find the example and the symbol of peace between nations and in the international relations of peoples.

LOVING OTHER CHRISTIANS IN THE LORD

*From a speech given while he served
as apostolic visitor in Bulgaria:*

If I were sure not to be misunderstood, I would like to address a word also to all our separated brothers. The difference in religious convictions with regard to one of the fundamental points of the teaching of Jesus recorded by the gospel, that is, the union of all the faithful of the church of Christ with the successor of the Prince of the Apostles, compelled me to observe a certain caution in my relations and personal contacts with them. This was quite natural, and I think perfectly understood by them too. The respect which I have always sought to show, in public and private, for all and every one of them, my unbreakable silence which hurt no one, and the fact that I never stooped to pick up the stone that was hurled at me from one or the other side of the street, leave me with the frank assurance that I showed them all that I love them too in the Lord, with that brotherly, sincere and heartfelt charity that we learn from the gospel.

Let us give serious thought to the salvation of our souls. That day will surely come when there will be one flock and one shepherd, because this is the will of Jesus Christ. Let us hasten with our prayers the coming of that blessed day. "Way of love, way of truth."

"I Am Joseph, Your Brother"

From the encyclical Ad Petri Cathedram
(On Truth, Unity and Peace, 88-90):

We address suppliant prayers to our gracious God, the giver of heavenly light and of all good things, that he safeguard the unity of the church and extend the fold and kingdom of Christ. We urge all our brethren in Christ and our beloved sons to pray fervently for the same intentions. The outcome of the approaching ecumenical council will depend more on a crusade of fervent prayer than on human effort and diligent application. And so with loving heart we also invite to this crusade all who are not of this fold but reverence and worship God and strive in good faith to obey his commands.

May the divine plea of Christ further and fulfill this hope and these prayers of ours: "Holy Father, keep in your name those whom you have given me, that they may be one even as we are. . . . Sanctify them in the truth. Your word is truth. . . . Yet not for these only do I pray, but for those also who through their word are to believe in me . . . that they may be perfected in unity. . . ." (John 17:11, 17, 20-21, 23).

We repeat this prayer, as does the whole Catholic world in union with us. We are spurred by a burning love for all men, but also by that interior humility which the gospel teaches. For we know the lowliness of him whom God raised to the dignity of the Sovereign Pontificate, not because of our merits, but according to his mysterious designs. Wherefore, to all our brethren and sons who are separated from the Chair of Blessed Peter, we say again: "I am . . . Joseph, your brother" (Genesis 45:4). Come, "make room for us" (2 Corinthians 7:2). We want nothing else, desire nothing else, pray God for nothing else but your salvation, your eternal happiness. ❧

THE MIRACLE OF LOVE

From a daily papal message:

That they may all be one; even as you, Father, are in me, and I in you, that they also may be in us, so that the world may believe that you have sent me (John 17:21).

This is the culmination of the miracle of love, which began at Bethlehem, and of which the shepherds and the Magi kings were the first fruits: the salvation of all men, their union in faith and love, through the visible church founded by Christ.

"That they may be one." This is the divine Redeemer's purpose, and we must do our best to further it, for it is a grave responsibility entrusted to every man's conscience. On the last day of the particular and universal judgment every individual will be asked, not whether he succeeded in restoring unity but whether he prayed, labored and suffered for it: whether he imposed upon himself a wise and prudent discipline, patient and farseeing, and whether he gave full scope to impulses of love.

This prayer from Christ's heart must persuade us to renew and intensify our efforts, so that all Catholics may continue faithfully to love, and to manifest the church's primary distinguishing mark, which is unity, and so that, in the vast and varied field of Christian denominations and beyond, there may be formed that unity so ardently desired by all honest and generous hearts.

O Eternal Word of the Father, Son of God and of Mary, renew once more in the secret depths of men's hearts the miracle of your birth! Re-clothe with immortality the children you have redeemed: make them aflame with charity, gather all together in the unity of your mystical body so that your coming may bring real joy, sure peace and the true brotherhood of individuals and peoples. Amen, amen. ༄

Unity in the Family

From the encyclical Ad Petri Cathedram
(On Truth, Unity and Peace, 50-58):

We have called nations, their rulers, and all classes of society to harmonious unity. Now we sincerely urge families to achieve and strengthen this unity within themselves.

For unless peace, unity, and concord are present in domestic society, how can they exist in civil society?

This harmonious unity which should exist within the family circle rises from the holiness and indissolubility of Christian marriage. It is the basis of much of the order, progress, and prosperity of civil society.

Within the family, the father stands in God's place. He must lead and guide the rest by his authority and the example of his good life.

The mother, on the other hand, should form her children firmly and graciously by the mildness of her manner and by her virtue.

Together the parents should carefully rear their children, God's most precious gift, to an upright and religious life.

Children must honor, obey, and love their parents. They must give their parents not only solace but also concrete assistance if it is needed.

The charity which burned in the household at Nazareth should be an inspiration for every family. All the Christian virtues should flourish in the family, unity should thrive, and the example of its virtuous living should shine brightly.

We earnestly pray God to prevent any damage to this valuable, beneficial, and necessary union. The Christian family is a sacred institution. If it totters, if the norms which the divine Redeemer laid down for it are rejected or ignored, then the very foundations of the state tremble; civil society stands betrayed and in peril. Everyone suffers. ❧

5

"Lord, Grant Us Your Peace"

In spite of the wars he had seen ravage his era and the increasing threat of nuclear destruction, Angelo Roncalli remained a man of optimism and trust in the Savior of the human race. His endeavors for peace were directed to all: the families and congregations he pastored; the international leaders he dealt with; and any anxious, restless men and women he met, whether their hearts were troubled and pained by their own sins or by the injustices of the societies in which they lived.

Roncalli knew that peace, "a gift of God beyond compare and the object of man's highest desire," requires truth, generosity, and good will. He urged men and women of all faiths to place their trust in God to find interior peace: "There can be no peace between men unless there is peace within each one of them." He challenged the world powers to disarm, insisting that true and solid peace among nations consists not in a balance of arms but in mutual trust, justice, and sincere cooperation. To many, Pope John XXIII became, as one commentator said, "a symbol of peace in a world on the edge of the abyss of total war."

At the height of the Cuban missile crisis in 1962, Pope John XXIII delivered a momentous radio address, appealing to the consciences of world leaders. "Hear the anguished cry which rises to heaven from every corner of the earth," he beseeched them, "from innocent children to old men, from the people in the cities and villages: Peace! Peace!" As newspapers around the world headlined his pleas, there was a marked lessening of the tension that had been building between East and West. Two days later, Chairman Khrushchev announced that the Russian missiles would be withdrawn from Cuba, and President Kennedy hailed Khrushchev for an act of statesmanship.

Pope John XXIII's encyclical *Pacem in Terris* (Peace on Earth) was his final gift to the world, issued shortly before his death. The "magnum opus" of his pontificate, the encyclical was the first to be addressed not only to bishops and Catholic faithful but "to all men of good will." The document represented a blueprint for a world community in which men of different religious and political persuasions could live in harmony, justice, security, and freedom. *The New York Times* called it "the most profound and all-embracing formulations of the road toward peace that has ever been written."

On May 10, 1963, Pope John was awarded the Balzan Peace Prize. As he was seriously ill, his doctors urged him not to attend the award ceremony. The pope replied, "But why not? What could be finer than for a father to die in the bosom of his assembled children?" ❧

PEACE IN THE HOME

From a daily papal message:

Peace is first found and enjoyed in the family, in a man's home. To obtain this we need understanding and generosity because even where there is mutual affection, there is always something to cause displeasure to one member or another. So patience is required, holy patience, the source of happiness; we must know how to correct our own characters, and moderate those desires which do not always conform to the divine law. The Redeemer came to teach us to live good honest lives as individuals, in our families and in the social order of cities, nations and the whole world.

The gift of peace is immensely precious for the human family. Every priest, every bishop, and the pope in particular, prays for this with great confidence in God. The good wishes of the Chief Shepherd and of all the other shepherds of God's church are in this: "Peace be with you!" and this prayer rises, ever more longing, and more widely spread throughout the world. The enthusiastic and magnificent response of all believers finds its expression in a vast program of labor and life. "But now in Christ Jesus you who were once far off have been brought near in the blood of Christ. For he is our peace" (Ephesians 2:13-14).

Peace to Men of Good Will

From a Christmas message,
delivered on December 23, 1959:

Peace is before all else an interior thing, belonging to the spirit, and its fundamental condition is a loving and filial dependence on the will of God. "You have made us for yourself, O Lord, and our heart is restless till it rests in you" (St. Augustine, *Confessions*, I, I).

All that weakens, that breaks, that destroys this conformity and union of wills is opposed to peace. First of all and before all is wrongdoing, sin. "Who has resisted him and has had peace?" (Job 9:4). Peace is the happy legacy of those who keep the divine law. "Much peace have they who love your law" (Psalms 119:165).

For its part, good will is only the sincere determination to respect the eternal laws of God, to conform oneself to his commandments and to follow his paths—in a word, to abide in the truth. This is the glory which God expects to receive from man. "Peace to men of good will."

The Personal Dignity of Man

Social peace is solidly based on the mutual and reciprocal respect for the personal dignity of man. The Son of God was made man, and his redeeming act concerns not only the collectivity, but also the individual man.

He "loved me and gave himself up for me" (Galatians 2:20). Thus spoke St. Paul to the Galatians. And if God has loved man to such a degree, that indicates that man is of interest to him and that the human person has an absolute right to be respected.

Such is the teaching of the church which, for the solution of these social questions, has always fixed her gaze on the human person and has taught that things and institutions—goods, the economy, the state—are primarily for man; not man for them.

The disturbances which unsettle the internal peace of nations trace their origins chiefly to this source: that man has been treated almost exclusively as a machine, a piece of merchandise, a worthless cog in some great machine or a mere productive unit.

It is only when the dignity of the person comes to be taken as the standard of value for man and his activities that the means will exist to settle civil discord and the often profound divisions between, for example, employers and the employed. Above all, it is only then that the means will exist to secure for the institution of the family those conditions of life, work and assistance which are capable of making it better directed to its function as a cell of society and the first community instituted by God himself for the development of the human person.

No peace will have solid foundations unless hearts nourish the sentiment of brotherhood which ought to exist among all who have a common origin and are called to the same destiny. The knowledge that they belong to the same family extinguishes lust, greed, pride, and the instinct to dominate others, which are the roots of dissensions and wars. It binds all in a single bond of higher and more fruitful solidarity.

The Basis of Peace Is Truth

The basis of international peace is, above all, truth. For in international relations, too, the Christian saying is valid: "The truth shall make you free" (John 8:32).

It is necessary, then, to overcome certain erroneous ideas: the myths of force, of nationalism or of other things that have prevented the integrated life of nations. And it is necessary to impose a peaceful living-together on moral principles, according to the teaching of right reason and of Christian doctrine.

Along with this, and enlightened by truth, should come justice. This removes the causes of quarrels and wars, solves the disputes, fixes the tasks, defines the duties and gives the answer to the claims of each party.

Justice in its turn ought to be integrated and sustained by Christian charity. That is, love for one's neighbor and one's own people ought not to be concentrated on one's self in an exclusive egotism which is suspicious of another's good. But it ought to expand and reach out spontaneously toward the community of interests, to embrace all peoples and to interweave common human relations. Thus it will be possible to speak of living together, and not of mere coexistence which, precisely because it is deprived of this inspiration of mutual dependence, raises barriers behind which nestle mutual suspicion, fear and terror.

A Gift Beyond Compare

Peace is a gift of God beyond compare. Likewise, it is the object of man's highest desire. It is moreover indivisible. None of the lineaments which make up its unmistakable appearance can be ignored or excluded.

In addition, since the men of our time have not completely carried into effect the conditions of peace, the result has been that God's paths toward peace have no meeting point with those of man. Hence there is the abnormal situation of this postwar period which has created, as it were, two blocs with all their uneasy conditions. There is not a state of war, but neither is there peace, the thing which the nations ardently desire.

At all times, because true peace is indivisible in its various aspects, it will not succeed in establishing itself on the social and international planes unless it is also, and in the first place, an interior fact. This requires then before all else—it is necessary to repeat—"men of good will." These are precisely those to whom the angels of Bethlehem announced peace: "Peace among men of good will" (Luke 2:14). Indeed they alone can give reality to the conditions contained in the definition of peace given by St. Thomas: the ordered harmony of citizens (*Contra Gentiles*, 3) and therefore order and harmony.

But how will true peace be able to put forth the twofold blossom of order and concord if the persons who hold positions of public responsibility, before selecting the advantages and risks of their decisions, fail to recognize themselves as persons subject to the eternal moral laws?

It will be necessary again and again to remove from the path the obstacles placed by the malice of man. And the presence of these obstacles is noted in the propaganda of immorality, in social injustice, in forced unemployment, in poverty contrasted with the luxury of those who can indulge in dissipation, in the dreadful lack of proportion between the technical and moral progress of nations, and in the unchecked armaments race. ☙

BANISHING THE FEAR OF WAR

From the encyclical Pacem in Terris
(Peace on Earth, 109-119):

We are deeply distressed to see the enormous stocks of armaments that have been, and continue to be, manufactured in the economically more developed countries. This policy is involving a vast outlay of intellectual and material resources, with the result that the people of these countries are saddled with a great burden, while other countries lack the help they need for their economic and social development.

There is a common belief that under modern conditions peace cannot be assured except on the basis of an equal balance of armaments and that this factor is the probable cause of this stockpiling of armaments. Thus, if one country increases its military strength, others are immediately roused by a competitive spirit to augment their own supply of armaments. And if one country is equipped with atomic weapons, others consider themselves justified in producing such weapons themselves, equal in destructive force.

Consequently people are living in the grip of constant fear. They are afraid that at any moment the impending storm may break upon them with horrific violence. And they have good reasons for their fear, for there is certainly no lack of such weapons. While it is difficult to believe that anyone would dare to assume responsibility for initiating the appalling slaughter and destruction that war would bring in its wake, there is no denying that the conflagration could be started by some chance and unforeseen circumstance. Moreover, even though the monstrous power of modern weapons does indeed act as a deterrent, there is reason to fear that the very testing of nuclear devices for war purposes can, if continued, lead to serious danger for various forms of life on earth.

Reducing the Stockpiles

Hence justice, right reason, and the recognition of man's dignity cry out insistently for a cessation to the arms race. The stockpiles of armaments which have been built up in various countries must be reduced all round and simultaneously by the parties concerned. Nuclear weapons must be banned. A general agreement must be reached on a suitable disarmament program, with an effective system of mutual control. In the words of Pope Pius XII: "The calamity of a world war, with the economic and social ruin and the moral excesses and dissolution that accompany it, must not on any account be permitted to engulf the human race for a third time."

Everyone, however, must realize that, unless this process of disarmament be thoroughgoing and complete, and reach men's very souls, it is impossible to stop the arms race, or to reduce armaments, or—and this is the main thing—ultimately to abolish them entirely. Everyone must sincerely cooperate in the effort to banish fear and the anxious expectation of war from men's minds. But this requires that the fundamental principles upon which peace is based in today's world be replaced by an altogether different one, namely, the realization that true and lasting peace among nations cannot consist in the possession of an equal supply of armaments but only in mutual trust. And we are confident that this can be achieved, for it is a thing which not only is dictated by common sense, but is in itself most desirable and most fruitful of good.

Protecting Our Destiny and Dignity

Here, then, we have an objective dictated first of all by reason. There is general agreement—or at least there should be—that relations between states, as between individuals, must be regulated not by armed force, but in accordance with the principles of right reason: the principles, that is, of truth, justice and vigorous and sincere cooperation.

Secondly, it is an objective which we maintain is more earnestly to be desired. For who is there who does not feel the craving to be rid of the threat of war, and to see peace preserved and made daily more secure?

And finally it is an objective which is rich with possibilities for good. Its advantages will be felt everywhere, by individuals, by families, by nations, by the whole human race. The warning of Pope Pius XII still rings in our ears: "Nothing is lost by peace; everything may be lost by war."

We therefore consider it our duty as the vicar on earth of Jesus Christ—Savior of the world, the Author of peace—and as interpreter of the most ardent wishes of the whole human family, in the fatherly love we bear all mankind, to beg and beseech mankind, and above all the rulers of states, to be unsparing of their labor and efforts to ensure that human affairs follow a rational and dignified course.

In their deliberations together, let men of outstanding wisdom and influence give serious thought to the problem of achieving a more human adjustment of relations between states throughout the world. It must be an adjustment that is based on mutual trust, sincerity in negotiation, and the faithful fulfillment of obligations assumed. Every aspect of the problem must be examined, so that eventually there may emerge some point of agreement from which to initiate treaties which are sincere, lasting, and beneficial in their effects.

We, for our part, will pray unceasingly that God may bless these labors by his divine assistance, and make them fruitful. ❧

WE ARE CALLED BROTHERS

From the encyclical Ad Petri Cathedram
(On Truth, Unity and Peace, 23-31):

God created men as brothers, not foes. He gave them the earth to be cultivated by their toil and labor. Each and every man is to enjoy the fruits of the earth and receive from it his sustenance and the necessities of life. The various nations are simply communities of men, that is, of brothers. They are to work in brotherly cooperation for the common prosperity of human society, not simply for their own particular goals.

Besides this, our journey through this mortal life should not be regarded as an end in itself, entered upon merely for pleasure. This journey leads beyond the burial of our human flesh to immortal life, to a fatherland which will endure forever.

If this teaching, this consoling hope, were taken away from men, there would be no reason for living. Lusts, dissensions, and disputes would erupt from within us. There would be no reasonable check to restrain them. The olive branch of peace would not shine in our thoughts; the firebrands of war would blaze there. Our lot would be cast with beasts, who do not have the use of reason. Ours would be an even worse lot, for we do have the use of reason and by abusing it (which, unfortunately, often happens) we can sink into a state lower than that of beasts. Like Cain, we would commit a terrible crime and stain the earth with our brother's blood.

Sharing a Common Destiny

Before all else, then, we must turn our thoughts to sound principles if we wish, as we should, to guide our actions along the path of justice.

We are called brothers. We actually are brothers. We share a common destiny in this life and the next. Why, then, do we act as though we are foes and enemies? Why do we envy one another? Why do we stir up hatred? Why do we ready lethal weapons for use against our brothers?

There has already been enough warfare among men! Too many youths in the flower of life have shed their blood already! Legions of the dead, all fallen in battle, dwell within this earth of ours. Their stern voices urge us all to return at once to harmony, unity, and a just peace.

All men, then, should turn their attention away from those things that divide and separate us, and should consider how they may be joined in mutual and just regard for one another's opinions and possessions.

Only if we desire peace, as we should, instead of war, and only if we all aspire sincerely to fraternal harmony among nations, shall it come to pass that public affairs and public questions are correctly understood and settled to the satisfaction of all. Then shall international conferences seek and reach decisions conducive to the longed-for unity of the whole human family. In the enjoyment of that unity, individual nations will see that their right to liberty is not subject to another's whims but is fully secure.

Those who oppress others and strip them of their due liberty can contribute nothing to the attainment of this unity. ∼

THE TRIUMPH OF GOD'S MERCY

From an address given as cardinal patriarch of Venice:

When every now and then, among the thorns of life, we find the Lord has set a spray of jasmine or a rose, or some other lovely flower, our hearts are filled with joy—but these little things cannot give us real peace. They are but a respite. St. Gregory the Great finely says that they are like a "little breathing space"; they are indeed a breath of peace, but of an armed peace that has to be defended . . . from temptations. The enjoyment of peace is something much more perfect. It depends on the triumph of the work of God's mercy in our souls. St. Augustine says: one hope, one faith, one promise: your mercy.

In Psalm 136 this mercy, this "steadfast love," is referred to no fewer than twenty-six times, for his mercy endures forever. And this is what strengthens us in the endeavor to preserve interior peace.

St. Leonard of Porto Maurizio has given us precious counsel on this theme: "In my midday examination of conscience I shall look briefly into my heart, to see whether it enjoys interior peace, founded on the holy will of God, so that I may confirm this peace if it should be imperiled. My Jesus, mercy. ༄

MY PEACE I GIVE YOU

From the encyclical Pacem in Terris
(Peace on Earth, 165, 170-171):

The world will never be the dwelling place of peace, till peace has found a home in the heart of each and every man, till every man preserves in himself the order ordained by God to be preserved. That is why St. Augustine asks the question: "Does your mind desire the strength to gain the mastery over your passions? Let it submit to a greater power, and it will conquer all beneath it. And peace will be in you—true, sure, most ordered peace. What is that order? God as ruler of the mind; the mind as ruler of the body. Nothing could be more orderly" (*Sermones post Maurinos reperti*).

The sacred liturgy of these days re-echoes the same message: "Our Lord Jesus Christ, after his resurrection stood in the midst of his disciples and said: Peace be upon you, alleluia. The disciples rejoiced when they saw the Lord." It is Christ, therefore, who brought us peace; Christ who bequeathed it to us: "Peace I leave with you; my peace I give to you: not as the world gives do I give to you" (John 14:27).

Let us, then, pray with all fervor for this peace which our divine Redeemer came to bring us. May he banish from the souls of men whatever might endanger peace. May he transform all men into witnesses of truth, justice and brotherly love. May he illumine with his light the minds of rulers, so that, besides caring for the proper material welfare of their peoples, they may also guarantee them the fairest gift of peace.

Finally, may Christ inflame the desires of all men to break through the barriers which divide them, to strengthen the bonds of mutual love, to learn to understand one another, and to pardon those who have done them wrong. Through his power and inspiration may all peoples welcome each other to their hearts as brothers, and may the peace they long for ever flower and ever reign among them.

"In the Bright Light of Truth"

For Pope John XXIII, truth was "the light which must irradiate our whole personality and set its mark on every act of our lives." It was a light that shone through Angelo Roncalli's thoughts and actions, his personal journal and correspondence, and his sermons and writings.

The essence and source of all truth is, of course, God. Pope John was convinced that if individuals, societies, and nations followed the truth and the precepts of the gospel, unity and peace would follow. He saw dissension and discord as stemming from one cause: ignorance of the truth.

In his personal life, Angelo Roncalli was thoroughly honest with himself and with God about his weaknesses and failings. In his letters to his family, he was genuine in his affection and in his concern to encourage them in their faith, not hesitating to "speak the truth in love" (Ephesians 4:15). His journal is filled with soul-searching, as he sought to root out the sin and falsehood in his life.

Truth was also a dominant theme of John XXIII's papacy. In his very first year as pope, he wrote the encyclical *Ad Petri Cathedram* (On Truth, Unity and Peace). Stressing responsibility to the truth, he declared in *Princeps Pastorum* (On the Missions, the Native

Clergy, and Lay Participation), "Anyone who deems himself a Christian must know that he is bound by his conscience to the basic, imperative duty of bearing witness to the truth in which he believes and to the grace which has transformed his soul" (34).

"The truth. Always the truth," he urged. "Speak it and write it with respect and care. Speak it to others as you would have it spoken to you. And do it always in such a way as not to offend the sacred meaning of divine or human law, of innocence, of justice, or of peace." ∾

FEED OUR MINDS ON TRUTH

From a daily papal message:

We must live in the truth: here all believers come face to face with the truth, which firmly and gently rules all men.

Christ's words, in fact, confront every man with his own responsibility, that is, his acceptance or rejection of the truth; they implore us most persuasively to remain in the truth, to feed our minds on truth and to act accordingly.

My message today . . . is a solemn appeal to you all to live in the truth, thus fulfilling your fourfold obligation of thinking, honoring, telling and doing what is true.

First of all then, *to think the truth*: to have clear notions of the great divine and human realities of redemption and of the church, of morality and of law, of philosophy and art; to have right ideas, or at least to try to form them conscientiously and with honest intention.

To honor the truth: this is an appeal to you to be shining examples in all spheres of individual, family, professional and social life. Truth makes us free; it ennobles those who profess it openly and without considering the opinion of the world. Why then should we be afraid to honor it, and to insist on its being treated with respect?

To tell the truth: this is what every mother teaches her child: to beware of telling lies. As the years pass telling the truth becomes second nature and makes the man of honor, the perfect Christian of frank and ready speech. And this is the testimony which the God of truth requires of every one of his children.

Finally, *to do everything according to the truth*: this is the light which must irradiate our whole personality and set its mark on every act of our lives. ❧

GOD IS THE FIRST TRUTH

From the encyclical Pacem in Terris
(Peace on Earth, 35-38):

Before a society can be considered well-ordered, creative, and consonant with human dignity, it must be based on truth. St. Paul expressed this as follows: "Putting away falsehood, let every one speak the truth with his neighbor, for we are members one of another" (Ephesians 4:25). And so will it be, if each man acknowledges sincerely his own rights and his own duties toward others.

Human society, as we here picture it, demands that men be guided by justice, respect the rights of others, and do their duty. It demands, too, that they be animated by such love as will make them feel the needs of others as their own, and induce them to share their goods with others, and to strive in the world to make all men alike heirs to the noblest of intellectual and spiritual values. Nor is this enough; for human society thrives on freedom, namely, on the use of means which are consistent with the dignity of its individual members, who, being endowed with reason, assume responsibility for their own actions.

And so, dearest sons and brothers, we must think of human society as being primarily a spiritual reality. By its means enlightened men can share their knowledge of the truth, can claim their rights and fulfill their duties, receive encouragement in their aspirations for the goods of the spirit, share their enjoyment of all the wholesome pleasures of the world, and strive continually to pass on to others all that is best in themselves and to make their own the spiritual riches of others. It is these spiritual values which exert a guiding influence on culture, economics, social institutions, political movements and forms, laws, and all the other components which go to make up the external community of men and its continual development.

The Moral Order of Society

Now the order which prevails in human society is wholly incorporeal in nature. Its foundation is truth, and it must be brought into effect by justice. It needs to be animated and perfected by men's love for one another, and, while preserving freedom intact, it must make for an equilibrium in society which is increasingly more human in character.

But such an order—universal, absolute and immutable in its principles—finds its source in the true, personal, and transcendent God. He is the first truth, the sovereign good, and as such the deepest source from which human society, if it is to be properly constituted, creative, and worthy of man's dignity, draws its genuine vitality. This is what St. Thomas means when he says: "Human reason is the standard which measures the degree of goodness of the human will, and as such it derives from the eternal law, which is divine reason . . . Hence it is clear that the goodness of the human will depends much more on the eternal law than on human reason" (*Summa Theologiae*, I-II).

MEN AND WOMEN CAN DISCOVER THE TRUTH

From the encyclical Ad Petri Cathedram
(*On Truth, Unity and Peace, 6-7, 9-12, 14-16, 19-21*):

All the evils which poison men and nations and trouble so many hearts have a single cause and a single source: ignorance of the truth—and at times even more than ignorance, a contempt for truth and a reckless rejection of it. Thus arise all manner of errors, which enter the recesses of men's hearts and the bloodstream of human society as would a plague. These errors turn everything upside down: they menace individuals and society itself.

And yet, God gave each of us an intellect capable of attaining natural truth. If we adhere to this truth, we adhere to God himself, the Author of truth, the Lawgiver and Ruler of our lives. But if we reject this truth, whether out of foolishness, neglect, or malice, we turn our backs on the highest good itself and on the very norm for right living. . . .

Attacks on the Truth

Some men, as the Apostle of the Gentiles warns us, are "ever learning yet never attaining knowledge of the truth" (2 Timothy 3:7). They contend that the human mind can discover no truth that is certain or sure; they reject the truths revealed by God and necessary for our eternal salvation.

Such men have strayed pathetically far from the teaching of Christ and the views expressed by the Apostle when he said, "Let us all attain to the unity of the faith and of the deep knowledge of the Son of God . . . that we may no longer be children, tossed to and fro and carried about by every wind of doctrine devised in the wickedness of men, in craftiness, according to the wiles of error. Rather are we to practice the truth in love, and grow up in all things in him who is the head, Christ. For from him the whole body (being closely joined and knit together through every joint of the system according to the functioning in due measure of each single part) derives its increase to the building up of itself in love" (Ephesians 4:13-16).

Anyone who consciously and wantonly attacks known truth, who arms himself with falsehood in his speech, his writings, or his conduct in order to attract and win over less learned men and to shape the inexperienced and impressionable minds of the young to his own way of thinking, takes advantage of the inexperience and innocence of others and engages in an altogether despicable business.

The Media Should Promote Truth

In this connection we must urge to careful, exact, and prudent presentation of the truth those especially who, through the books, magazines, and daily newspapers which are so abundant today, have such a great effect on the instruction and development of the minds of men, and especially of the young, and play such a large part in forming their opinions and shaping their characters. These people have a serious duty to disseminate not lies, error, and obscenity, but only the truth; they are particularly bound to publicize what is conducive to good and virtuous conduct, not to vice. . . .

And in this day of ours, as you well know, venerable brothers and beloved sons, we also have radio broadcasts, motion pictures, and television (which can enter easily into the home). All of these can provide inspiration and incentive for morality and goodness, even Christian virtue. Unfortunately, however, they can also entice men, especially the young, to loose morality and ignoble behavior, to treacherous error and perilous vice.

The weapons of truth, then, must be used in defense against these weapons of evil. We must strive zealously and relentlessly to ward off the impact of this great evil which every day insinuates itself more deeply.

We must fight immoral and false literature with literature that is wholesome and sincere. Radio broadcasts, motion pictures, and television shows which make error and vice attractive must be opposed by shows which defend truth and strive to preserve the integrity and safety of morals. Thus these new arts, which can work much evil, will be turned to the well-being and benefit of men, and at the same time will supply worthwhile recreation. Health will come from a source which has often produced only devastating sickness. . . .

Attaining the Truth in Its Fullness

So much toil and effort is expended today in mastering and advancing human knowledge that our age glories—and rightly—in the amazing progress it has made in the field of scientific research. But why do we not devote as much energy, ingenuity, and enthusiasm to the sure and safe attainment of that learning which concerns not this earthly, mortal life but the life which lies ahead of us in heaven? Our spirit will rest in peace and joy only when we have reached that truth which is taught in the gospels and which should be reduced to action in our lives. This is a joy which surpasses by far any pleasure which can come from the study of things human or from those marvelous inventions which we use today and are constantly praising to the skies.

Once we have attained the truth in its fullness, integrity, purity, and unity should pervade our minds, hearts, and actions. For there is only one cause of discord, disagreement, and dissension: ignorance of the truth, or what is worse, rejection of the truth once it has been sought and found. It may be that the truth is rejected because of the practical advantages which are expected to result from false views; it may be that it is rejected as a result of that perverted blindness which seeks easy and indulgent excuses for vice and immoral behavior.

All men, therefore, private citizens as well as government officials, must love the truth sincerely if they are to attain that peace and harmony on which depends all real prosperity, public and private. ✍

FINDING OURSELVES IN GOD

From the encyclical Mater et Magistra
(Mother and Teacher, 214-215, 239):

The most fundamental modern error is that of imagining that man's natural sense of religion is nothing more than the outcome of feeling or fantasy, to be eradicated from his soul as an anachronism and an obstacle to human progress. And yet this very need for religion reveals a man for what he is: a being created by God and tending always toward God. As we read in St. Augustine: "Lord, you have made us for yourself, and our hearts can find no rest until they rest in you" (*Confessions*, I, I).

Let men make all the technical and economic progress they can, there will be no peace nor justice in the world until they return to a sense of their dignity as creatures and sons of God, who is the first and final cause of all created being. Separated from God a man is but a monster, in himself and toward others; for the right ordering of human society presupposes the right ordering of man's conscience with God, who is himself the source of all justice, truth and love. . . .

In their economic and social activities, Catholics often come into contact with others who do not share their view of life. In such circumstances, they must, of course, bear themselves as Catholics and do nothing to compromise religion and morality. Yet at the same time they should show themselves animated by a spirit of understanding and unselfishness, ready to cooperate loyally in achieving objectives which are good in themselves, or can be turned to good.

THE DEMANDS OF TRUTH

From the encyclical Pacem in Terris
(Peace on Earth, 86-90):

Mutual ties between states must be governed by truth. Truth calls for the elimination of every trace of racial discrimination, and the consequent recognition of the inviolable principle that all states are by nature equal in dignity.

Each of them accordingly has the right to exist, to develop, and to possess the necessary means and accept a primary responsibility for its own development. Each is also legitimately entitled to its good name and to the respect which is its due.

As we know from experience, men frequently differ widely in knowledge, virtue, intelligence, and wealth, but that is no valid argument in favor of a system whereby those who are in a position of superiority impose their will arbitrarily on others. On the contrary, such men have a greater share in the common responsibility to help others to reach perfection by their mutual efforts.

So, too, on the international level: some nations may have attained to a superior degree of scientific, cultural, and economic development. But that does not entitle them to exert unjust political domination over other nations. It means that they have to make a greater contribution to the common cause of social progress.

Equal in Dignity

The fact is that no one can be by nature superior to his fellows, since all men are equally noble in natural dignity. And consequently there are no differences at all between political communities from the point of view of natural dignity. Each state is like a body, the members of which are human beings. And, as we know from experience, nations can be highly sensitive in matters in any way touching their dignity and honor; and with good reason.

Truth further demands an attitude of unrufffled impartiality in the use of the many aids to the promotion and spread of mutual understanding between nations which modern scientific progress has made available. This does not mean that people should be prevented from drawing particular attention to the virtues of their own way of life, but it does mean the utter rejection of ways of disseminating information which violate the principles of truth and justice, and injure the reputation of another nation. ∽

JESUS, THE ESSENCE AND SPLENDOR OF TRUTH

From a daily papal message:

St. Augustine gives a name to the divine Word which appeared at Bethlehem: he calls him the Truth, because he is the Only-begotten of the Father, shining in all the glory of his divine nature to enlighten the whole created world, visible and invisible, material and spiritual, human and superhuman.

The two Testaments contain the revelation of a doctrine which is from eternity, the essence and splendor of truth, shining through all the ages and revealed to man, because he is considered the masterpiece and high priest of the visible world. It is truly the living substantial doctrine of development of both the natural and supernatural orders.

In fact the first words of the Old Testament describe the origin of the world; the last words of the New Testament, "Come, Lord Jesus," are the summary of the whole history of law and grace.

It is natural that the souls created by God and destined for eternal life should seek to discover the truth, the primary object of the human mind's activity. Why must we speak the truth? Because truth comes from God, and between man and the truth there is no merely accidental relationship but one which is necessary and essential.

The Dawn of the
Second Vatican Council

On January 25, 1959, three months after his election, John XXIII surprised the church and the world by announcing his plan to convene an ecumenical council. The Second Vatican Council was the twenty-first such gathering held in the two-thousand-year life of the church and the first since 1870.

While past councils had been held to defend the Catholic faith against heresy or to define doctrines, Pope John envisioned that this council would bring vitality to the church in the modern world. Once, when asked what he expected the council to do, Pope John strode over to a window in his study and threw it open. "We expect the council to let some fresh air in here," he replied.

The pope called for a spirit of *aggiornamento*, a renewal that would affect the life and worship of every Catholic, a regeneration that would direct the church toward the unity of the Christian people, an impetus that would bring the truths of the faith and the teachings of the church to bear on modern society.

The Second Vatican Council was forty-five months in preparation. Pope John XXIII imposed no program on it, but established ten commissions to study particular questions in advance as well as a central commission to coordinate their efforts. In addition, all the bishops were asked to submit their proposals for subjects to be raised in the council sessions. Most were concerned with the pastoral needs of the church and also showed a great desire for ecumenical dialogue with Orthodox and non-Catholic Christians. Throughout these years of preparation, John XXIII urged all to intercede for the council, asking the clergy and laity, especially children, to offer their prayers and sacrifices.

More than twenty-six hundred bishops—the council Fathers—were present when the Second Vatican Council opened in October 1962. Thirty delegate-observers representing seventeen Christian denominations were also present, invited at the initiative of the ecumenically-minded pope. To these delegates John XXIII later said, "If you would but read my heart you will understand more than words can say." When the final session of the council convened in 1965, ninety-three observers were in attendance.

Already seriously ill with inoperable cancer during the first session of the council, John XXIII knew he would not live to see the next session. However, he was content to have opened the way for the action of the Holy Spirit. Looking ahead, he prophesied "a new Pentecost indeed, which will cause the church to renew her interior riches and to extend her maternal care in every sphere of human activity." ∽

As the Council Draws Near

From the encyclical Paenitentiam Agere
*(On the Need for the Practice of Interior and
Exterior Penance, 3-4, 22-25, 34, 38):*

And now, as the day for the opening of the Second Vatican Council draws nearer, we wish to repeat that request of ours [for prayer and voluntary sacrifice on behalf of the council] and dwell on it at greater length. In doing so we are confident that we are serving the best interests of this most important and solemn assembly. For while admitting that Christ is present to his church "all days, even unto the consummation of the world" (Matthew 28:20), we must think of him as being even closer to men's hearts and minds during the time of an ecumenical council, for he is present in the persons of his legates, of whom he said quite emphatically: "He who hears you, hears me" (Luke 10:16).

The ecumenical council will be a meeting of the successors of the apostles, men to whom the Savior of the human race gave the command to teach all nations and urge them to observe all his commandments (cf. Matthew 28:19-20). Its manifest task, therefore, will be publicly to reaffirm God's rights over mankind, whom Christ's blood has redeemed, and to reaffirm the duties of redeemed mankind towards its God and Savior. . . .

Prayerful Preparation

We too, venerable brethren, on the example of our predecessors, are most anxious that the whole Catholic world, both clerical and lay, shall prepare itself for this great event, the forthcoming council, by ardent prayer, good works, and the practice of Christian penance.

Clearly the most efficacious kind of prayer for gaining the divine protection is prayer that is offered publicly by the whole community; for our Redeemer said: "Where two or three are gathered together for my sake, there am I in the midst of them" (Matthew 18:20).

The situation, therefore, demands that Christians today, as in the days of the early church, shall be of "one heart and one soul" (Acts 4:32), imploring God with prayer and penance to grant that this great assembly may measure up to all our expectations.

The salutary results we pray for are these: that the faith, the love, the moral lives of Catholics may be so re-invigorated, so intensified, that all who are at present separated from this Apostolic See may be impelled to strive actively and sincerely for union. . . .

Finally, the object of the ecumenical council, as everyone knows, will be to render more effective that divine work which our Redeemer accomplished. Christ our Lord accomplished it by being "offered . . . because it was his own will" (Isaiah 53:7). He accomplished it not merely by teaching men his heavenly doctrine, but also, and more especially, by pouring out his most precious blood for their salvation. Yet each of us can say with St. Paul: "I now rejoice in my sufferings . . . and fill up those things that are wanting of the sufferings of Christ, in my flesh, for his body, which is the church" (Colossians 1:24). . . .

The "good seed" which the council will scatter far and wide over the church in those days must not be allowed to go to waste; it must find its way into hearts that are ready and prepared, loyal and true. If such is the case, then the forthcoming council will indeed be for the faithful, a fruitful source of eternal salvation. ∾

THE LONGED-FOR DAY DAWNS

Pope John XXIII addressed the bishops and observers at the opening session of the Second Vatican Council on October 11, 1962, in St. Peter's Basilica:

Mother Church rejoices that, by the singular gift of Divine Providence, the longed-for day has finally dawned when—under the auspices of the virgin Mother of God, whose maternal dignity is commemorated on this feast—the Second Vatican Ecumenical Council is being solemnly opened here beside St. Peter's tomb.

The councils—both the twenty ecumenical ones and the numberless others, also important, of a provincial or regional character which have been held down through the years—all prove clearly the vigor of the Catholic Church and are recorded as shining lights in her annals. . . .

Side by side with these motives for spiritual joy, however, there has also been for more than nineteen centuries a cloud of sorrows and of trials. Not without reason did the ancient Simeon announce to Mary the mother of Jesus, that prophecy which has been and still is true: "Behold this child is set for the fall and the resurrection of many in Israel, and for a sign which shall be contradicted" (Luke 2:34). And Jesus himself, when he grew up, clearly outlined the manner in which the world would treat his person down through the succeeding centuries with the mysterious words: "He who hears you, hears me" (10:16), and with those others that the same Evangelist relates: "He who is not with me is against me and he who does not gather with me scatters"(11:23).

For Him or Against Him

The great problem confronting the world after almost two thousand years remains unchanged. Christ is ever resplendent as the center of history and of life. Men are either with him and his church, and then they enjoy light, goodness, order, and peace. Or else they are without him, or against him, and deliberately opposed to his church, and then they give rise to confusion, to bitterness in human relations, and to the constant danger of fratricidal wars.

Ecumenical councils, whenever they are assembled, are a solemn celebration of the union of Christ and his church, and hence lead to the universal radiation of truth, to the proper guidance of individuals in domestic and social life, to the strengthening of spiritual energies for a perennial uplift toward real and everlasting goodness.

The testimony of this extraordinary magisterium of the church in the succeeding epochs of these twenty centuries of Christian history stands before us collected in numerous and imposing volumes, which are the sacred patrimony of our ecclesiastical archives, here in Rome and in the more noted libraries of the entire world.

The Unexpected Inspiration

As regards the initiative for the great event which gathers us here, it will suffice to repeat as historical documentation our personal account of the first sudden bringing up in our heart and lips of the simple words, "ecumenical council." We uttered those words in the presence of the Sacred College of Cardinals on that memorable January 25, 1959, the feast of the Conversion of St. Paul, in the basilica dedicated to him. It was completely unexpected, like a flash of heavenly light, shedding sweetness in eyes and hearts. And at the same time it gave rise to a great fervor throughout the world in expectation of the holding of the council.

There have elapsed three years of laborious preparation, during which a wide and profound examination was made regarding modern conditions of faith and religious practice, and of Christian and especially Catholic vitality. These years have seemed to us a first sign, an initial gift of celestial grace.

Illuminated by the light of this council, the church—
we confidently trust—will become greater in spiritual
riches and gaining the strength of new energies there-
from, she will look to the future without fear. In fact, by
bringing herself up to date where required, and by the
wise organization of mutual cooperation, the church will
make men, families, and peoples really turn their minds
to heavenly things.

And thus the holding of the council becomes a
motive for wholehearted thanksgiving to the Giver of
every good gift, in order to celebrate with joyous canti-
cles the glory of Christ our Lord, the glorious and
immortal King of ages and of peoples.

The opportuneness of holding the council is, moreover,
venerable brothers, another subject which it is useful to
propose for your consideration. Namely, in order to render our joy more complete, we wish to narrate before this
great assembly our assessment of the happy circumstances under which the ecumenical council commences.

Against the "Prophets of Gloom"

In the daily exercise of our pastoral office, we sometimes have to listen, much to our regret, to voices of persons who, though burning with zeal, are not endowed
with too much sense of discretion or measure. In these
modern times they can see nothing but prevarication and
ruin. They say that our era, in comparison with past eras,
is getting worse, and they behave as though they had
learned nothing from history, which is, nonetheless, the
teacher of life. They behave as though at the time of for-

mer councils everything was a full triumph for the Christian idea and life and for proper religious liberty.

We feel we must disagree with those prophets of gloom, who are always forecasting disaster, as though the end of the world were at hand.

In the present order of things, divine Providence is leading us to a new order of human relations which, by men's own efforts and even beyond their very expectations, are directed toward the fulfillment of God's superior and inscrutable designs. And everything, even human differences, leads to the greater good of the church.

The World of Today

It is easy to discern this reality if we consider attentively the world of today, which is so busy with politics and controversies in the economic order that it does not find time to attend to the care of spiritual reality, with which the church's magisterium is concerned. Such a way of acting is certainly not right, and must justly be disapproved. It cannot be denied, however, that these new conditions of modern life have at least the advantage of having eliminated those innumerable obstacles by which, at one time, the sons of this world impeded the free action of the church.

In fact, it suffices to leaf even cursorily through the pages of ecclesiastical history to note clearly how the ecumenical councils themselves, while constituting a series of true glories for the Catholic Church, were often held to the accompaniment of most serious difficulties and sufferings because of the undue interference of civil authorities. The princes of this world, indeed, sometimes in all sincerity, intended thus to protect the church. But more frequently this occurred not without spiritual damage and danger, since their interest therein was guided by the views of a selfish and perilous policy.

In this regard, we confess to you that we feel most poignant sorrow over the fact that very many bishops, so dear to us, are noticeable here today by their absence, because they are imprisoned for their faithfulness to Christ, or impeded by other restraints. The thought of them impels us to raise most fervent prayer to God. Nevertheless, we see today, not without great hopes and to our immense consolation, that the church, finally freed from so many obstacles of a profane nature such as trammeled her in the past, can from this Vatican Basilica, as if from a second apostolic cenacle, and through your intermediary, raise her voice resonant with majesty and greatness.

Guarding the Truth

The greatest concern of the ecumenical council is this: that the sacred deposit of Christian doctrine should be guarded and taught more efficaciously. That doctrine embraces the whole of man, composed as he is of body and soul. And, since he is a pilgrim on this earth, it commands him to tend always toward heaven.

This demonstrates how our mortal life is to be ordered in such a way as to fulfill our duties as citizens of earth and of heaven, and thus to attain the aim of life as established by God. That is, all men, whether taken singly or as united in society, today have the duty of tending ceaselessly during their lifetime toward the attainment of heavenly things and to use, for this purpose only, the earthly goods, the employment of which must not prejudice their eternal happiness.

The Lord has said: "Seek first the kingdom of God and his justice" (Matthew 6:33). The word "first" expresses the direction in which our thoughts and energies must move. We must not, however, neglect the other words of this exhortation of our Lord, namely: "And all these things shall be given you besides." In reality, there always have been in the church, and there are still today, those who, while seeking the practice of evangelical perfection with all their might, do not fail to make themselves useful to society. Indeed, it is from their constant example of life and their charitable undertakings that all that is highest and noblest in human society takes its strength and growth.

Looking to the Present

In order, however, that this doctrine may influence the numerous fields of human activity, with reference to individuals, to families, and to social life, it is necessary first of all that the church should never depart from the sacred patrimony of truth received from the Fathers. But at the same time she must ever look to the present, to the new conditions and new forms of life introduced into the modern world, which have opened new avenues to the Catholic apostolate.

For this reason, the church has not watched inertly the marvelous progress of the discoveries of human genius, and has not been backward in evaluating them rightly. But, while following these developments, she does not neglect to admonish men so that, over and above sense—perceived things—they may raise their eyes to God, the source of all wisdom and all beauty. And may they never forget the most serious command: "The Lord your God shall you worship, and him only shall you serve" (Matthew 4:10; Luke 4:8), so that it may happen that the fleeting fascination of visible things should impede true progress.

The Treasures of the Church

The manner in which sacred doctrine is spread, this having been established, it becomes clear how much is expected from the council in regard to doctrine. That is, the Twenty-first Ecumenical Council, which will draw upon the effective and important wealth of juridical, liturgical, apostolic, and administrative experiences, wishes to transmit the doctrine, pure and integral, without any attenuation or distortion, which throughout twenty centuries, notwithstanding difficulties and contrasts, has become the common patrimony of men. It is a patrimony not well received by all, but always a rich treasure available to men of good will.

Our duty is not only to guard this precious treasure, as if we were concerned only with antiquity, but to dedicate ourselves with an earnest will and without fear to that work which our era demands of us, pursuing thus the path which the church has followed for twenty centuries. The salient point of this council is not, therefore, a discussion of one article or another of the fundamental doctrine of the church which has repeatedly been taught by the Fathers and by ancient and modern theologians, and which is presumed to be well known and familiar to all.

For this a council was not necessary. But from the renewed, serene, and tranquil adherence to all the teaching of the church in its entirety and preciseness, as it still shines forth in the Acts of the Council of Trent and First Vatican Council, the Christian, Catholic, and apostolic spirit of the whole world expects a step forward toward a doctrinal penetration and a formation of consciousness in faithful and perfect conformity to the authentic doctrine, which, however, should be studied and expounded through the methods of research and through the literary forms of modern thought. The substance of the ancient doctrine of the deposit of faith is one thing, and the way in which it is presented is another. And it is the latter that must be taken into great consideration with patience if necessary, everything being measured in the forms and proportions of a magisterium which is predominantly pastoral in character.

The Medicine of Mercy

At the outset of the Second Vatican Council, it is evident, as always, that the truth of the Lord will remain forever. We see, in fact, as one age succeeds another, that the opinions of men follow one another and exclude each other. And often errors vanish as quickly as they arise, like fog before the sun. The church has always opposed these errors. Frequently she has condemned them with the greatest severity. Nowadays however, the Spouse of Christ prefers to make use of the medicine of mercy rather than that of severity. She considers that she meets the needs of the present day by demonstrating the validity of her teaching rather than by condemnations—not, certainly, that there is a lack of fallacious teaching, opinions, and dangerous concepts to be guarded against and dissipated. But these are so obviously in contrast with the right norm of honesty, and have produced such lethal fruits that by now it would seem that men of themselves are inclined to condemn them, particularly those ways of life which despise God and his law or place excessive confidence in technical progress and a well-being based exclusively on the comforts of life. They are ever more deeply convinced of the paramount dignity of the human person and of his perfection as well as of the duties which that implies. Even more important, experience has taught men that violence inflicted on others, the might of arms, and political domination, are of no help at all in finding a happy solution to the grave problems which afflict them.

A Loving Mother

That being so, the Catholic Church, raising the torch of religious truth by means of this ecumenical council, desires to show herself to be the loving mother of all, benign, patient, full of mercy and goodness toward the brethren who are separated from her. To mankind, oppressed by so many difficulties, the church says, as Peter said to the poor who begged alms from him: "I have neither gold nor silver, but what I have I give you; in the name of Jesus Christ of Nazareth, rise and walk" (Acts 3:6). In other words, the church does not offer to the men of today riches that pass, nor does she promise them merely earthly happiness. But she distributes to them the goods of divine grace which, raising men to the dignity of sons of God, are the most efficacious safeguards and aids toward a more human life. She opens the fountain of her life-giving doctrine which allows men, enlightened by the light of Christ, to understand well what they really are, what their lofty dignity and their purpose are, and, finally, through her children, she spreads everywhere the fullness of Christian charity, than which nothing is more effective in eradicating the seeds of discord, nothing more efficacious in promoting concord, just peace, and the brotherly unity of all.

The Unity of Christ

The church's solicitude to promote and defend truth derives from the fact that, according to the plan of God, who wills all men to be saved and to come to the knowledge of the truth (cf. 1 Timothy 2:4), men without the assistance of the whole of revealed doctrine cannot reach a complete and firm unity of minds, with which are associated true peace and eternal salvation.

Unfortunately, the entire Christian family has not yet fully attained this visible unity in truth.

The Catholic Church, therefore, considers it her duty

to work actively so that there may be fulfilled the great mystery of that unity, which Jesus Christ invoked with fervent prayer from his heavenly Father on the eve of his sacrifice. She rejoices in peace, knowing well that she is intimately associated with that prayer, and then exults greatly at seeing that invocation extend its efficacy with salutary fruit, even among those who are outside her fold.

Indeed, if one considers well this same unity which Christ implored for his church, it seems to shine, as it were, with a triple ray of beneficent supernal light: namely, the unity of Catholics among themselves, which must always be kept exemplary and most firm; the unity of prayers and ardent desires with which those Christians separated from this Apostolic See aspire to be united with us; and the unity in esteem and respect for the Catholic Church which animates those who follow non-Christian religions.

The Light of the Church

In this regard, it is a source of considerable sorrow to see that the greater part of the human race—although all men who are born were redeemed by the blood of Christ—does not yet participate in those sources of divine grace which exist in the Catholic Church. Hence the church, whose light illumines all, whose strength of supernatural unity redounds to the advantage of all humanity, is rightly described in these beautiful words of St. Cyprian:

> The church, surrounded by divine light, spreads her rays over the entire earth. This light, however, is one and unique and shines everywhere without

causing any separation in the unity of the body. She extends her branches over the whole world. By her fruitfulness she sends ever farther afield her rivulets. Nevertheless, the head is always one, the origin one for she is the one mother, abundantly fruitful. We are born of her, are nourished by her milk, we live of her spirit. (*De Catholicae Eccles. Unitate*, 5)

Venerable brothers, such is the aim of the Second Vatican Ecumenical Council, which, while bringing together the church's best energies and striving to have men welcome more favorably the good tidings of salvation, prepares, as it were and consolidates the path toward that unity of mankind which is required as a necessary foundation, in order that the earthly city may be brought to the resemblance of that heavenly city where truth reigns, charity is the law, and whose extent is eternity (cf. St. Augustine, *Epistle* 138, 3).

Now, "our voice is directed to you" (2 Corinthians 6:11), venerable brothers in the episcopate. Behold, we are gathered together in this Vatican Basilica, upon which hinges the history of the church where heaven and earth are closely joined, here near the tomb of Peter and near so many of the tombs of our holy predecessors, whose ashes in this solemn hour seem to thrill in mystic exultation.

The Council Rises like Daybreak

The council now beginning rises in the church like daybreak, a forerunner of most splendid light. It is now only dawn. And already at this first announcement of the rising day, how much sweetness fills our heart. Everything here breathes sanctity and arouses great joy. Let us contemplate the stars, which with their brightness augment the majesty of this temple. These stars, according to the testimony of the apostle John (cf. Revelation 1:20), are you, and with you we see shining around the tomb of the Prince of the Apostles, the golden candelabra. That is, the church is confided to you.

We see here with you important personalities, present in an attitude of great respect and cordial expectation, having come together in Rome from the five continents to represent the nations of the world.

We might say that heaven and earth are united in the holding of the council—the saints of heaven to protect our work, the faithful of the earth continuing in prayer to the Lord, and you, seconding the inspiration of the Holy Spirit in order that the work of all may correspond to the modern expectations and needs of the various peoples of the world.

This requires of you serenity of mind, brotherly concord, moderation in proposals, dignity in discussion, and wisdom of deliberation.

God grant that your labors and your work, toward which the eyes of all peoples and the hopes of the entire world are turned, may abundantly fulfill the aspirations of all.

Confidence in God

Almighty God! In you we place all our confidence, not trusting in our own strength. Look down benignly upon these pastors of your church. May the light of your supernal grace aid us in making decisions and in making laws. Graciously hear the prayers which we pour forth to you in unanimity of faith, of voice, and of mind.

O Mary, Help of Christians, Help of bishops, of whose love we have recently had particular proof in your temple of Loreto, where we venerated the mystery of the Incarnation, dispose all things for a happy and propitious outcome and, with your spouse, St. Joseph, the holy apostles Peter and Paul, St. John the Baptist, and St. John the Evangelist, intercede for us to God.

To Jesus Christ, our most amiable Redeemer, immortal King of peoples and of times, be love, power, and glory forever and ever.

The Fruits of the Council

As he battled inoperable intestinal cancer, Pope John XXIII said, "Now I understand what contribution to the council the Lord requires from me: suffering." Content to have "opened the windows," he trusted the Holy Spirit to bring to fulfillment and completion in the church what had been begun at the opening session of the Second Vatican Council. With fortitude and humility, he offered his physical pain and his death agony for those things dear to his heart: unity among Christians and the work of the council Fathers.

John's successor, Pope Paul VI, guided the council from its second session in the fall of 1963 through its fourth and final session, which ended on December 8, 1965. The day before its closing, the council Fathers witnessed a dramatic demonstration of ecumenism when Pope Paul and the Orthodox Patriarch, Athenagoras I, formally expressed their regret for the mutual excommunications pronounced by their predecessors, Pope Leo IX and Patriarch Cerularius, in 1054.

The Second Vatican Council produced sixteen documents that have continued to give focus and direction to the church through the years since they were written. The passages included in this chapter, though only a small fraction of what was actually produced by the council, highlight the fruits of the great process that had been set in motion under the inspiration of Pope John XXIII. ❧

THE CHURCH IN THE MODERN WORLD

Pope John often spoke of updating (aggiornamento) *the church, and believed that the church, through the council, could contribute more effectively to solving the problems presented by the modern age. One of the most important documents of the council,* Gaudium et Spes (*Pastoral Constitution on the Church in the Modern World*), *underscored the dignity of the human person and the importance of a relationship between the world and "a living and active" church. Excerpts are taken from paragraphs 1-4, 10, and 41.*

The joys and the hopes, the griefs and the anxieties of the men of this age, especially those who are poor or in any way afflicted, these are the joys and hopes, the griefs and anxieties of the followers of Christ. Indeed, nothing genuinely human fails to raise an echo in their hearts. For theirs is a community composed of men. United in Christ, they are led by the Holy Spirit in their journey to the kingdom of their Father and they have welcomed the news of salvation which is meant for every man. That is why this community realizes that it is truly linked with mankind and its history by the deepest of bonds.

Hence this Second Vatican Council, having probed more profoundly into the mystery of the church, now addresses itself without hesitation, not only to the sons of the church and to all who invoke the name of Christ, but to the whole of humanity. For the council yearns to explain to everyone how it conceives of the presence and activity of the church in the world of today.

Therefore, the council focuses its attention on the world of men, the whole human family along with the sum of those realities in the midst of which it lives; that world which is the theater of man's history, and the heir of his energies, his tragedies and his triumphs; that world which the Christian sees as created and sustained by its Maker's love, fallen indeed into the bondage of sin, yet emancipated now by Christ, who was crucified and rose again to break the strangle hold of personified evil, so that the world might be fashioned anew according to God's design and reach its fulfillment.

Engaged in Conversation

Though mankind is stricken with wonder at its own discoveries and its power, it often raises anxious questions about the current trend of the world, about the place and role of man in the universe, about the meaning of its individual and collective strivings, and about the ultimate destiny of reality and of humanity. Hence, giving witness and voice to the faith of the whole people of God gathered together by Christ, this council can provide no more eloquent proof of its solidarity with, as well as its respect and love for the entire human family with which it is bound up, than by engaging with it in conversation about these various problems. The council brings to mankind light kindled from the gospel, and puts at its disposal those saving resources which the church herself, under the guidance of the Holy Spirit, receives from her Founder. For the human person deserves to be preserved; human society deserves to be renewed. Hence the focal point of our total presentation will be man himself, whole and entire, body and soul, heart and conscience, mind and will.

Therefore, this sacred synod, proclaiming the noble destiny of man and championing the godlike seed which has been sown in him, offers to mankind the honest assistance of the church in fostering that brotherhood of all men which corresponds to this destiny of theirs. Inspired by no earthly ambition, the church seeks but a solitary goal: to carry forward the work of Christ under the lead of the befriending Spirit. And Christ entered this world to give witness to the truth, to rescue and not to sit in judgment, to serve and not to be served (cf. John 18:37; Matthew 20:28; Mark 10:45).

Discerning the Signs

The church has always had the duty of scrutinizing the signs of the times and of interpreting them in the light of the gospel. Thus, in language intelligible to each generation, she can respond to the perennial questions which men ask about this present life and the life to come, and about the relationship of the one to the other. We must therefore recognize and understand the world in which we live, its expectations, its longings, and its often dramatic characteristics. Some of the main features of the modern world can be sketched as follows.

Today, the human race is involved in a new stage of history. Profound and rapid changes are spreading by degrees around the whole world. Triggered by the intelligence and creative energies of man, these changes recoil upon him, upon his decisions and desires, both individual and collective, and upon his manner of thinking and acting with respect to things and to people. Hence we can already speak of a true cultural and social transformation, one which has repercussions on man's religious life as well. . . .

Nevertheless, in the face of the modern development of the world, the number constantly swells of the people who raise the most basic questions or recognize them with a new sharpness: What is man? What is this sense of sorrow, of evil, of death, which continues to exist despite so much progress? What purpose have these victories purchased at so high a cost? What can man offer to society, what can he expect from it? What follows this earthly life?

The church firmly believes that Christ, who died and was raised up for all (cf. 2 Corinthians 5:15), can through his Spirit offer man the light and the strength to measure up to his supreme destiny. Nor has any other name under the heaven been given to man by which it is fitting for him to be saved (cf. Acts 4:12). She likewise holds that in her most benign Lord and Master can be found the key, the focal point and the goal of man, as well as of all human history. The church also maintains that beneath all changes there are many realities which do not change and which have their ultimate foundation in Christ, who is the same yesterday and today, yes and forever (cf. Hebrews 13:8). Hence under the light of Christ, the image of the unseen God, the firstborn of every creature (cf. Colossians 1:15), the council wishes to speak to all men in order to shed light on the mystery of man and to cooperate in finding the solution to the outstanding problems of our time. . . .

The Rights of Men and Women

Modern man is on the road to a more thorough development of his own personality, and to a growing discovery and vindication of his own rights. Since it has been entrusted to the church to reveal the mystery of God, who is the ultimate goal of man, she opens up to man at the same time the meaning of his own existence, that is, the innermost truth about himself. The church truly knows that only God, whom she serves, meets the deepest longings of the human heart, which is never fully satisfied by what this world has to offer.

She also knows that man is constantly worked upon by God's Spirit, and hence can never be altogether indifferent to the problems of religion. The experience of past ages proves this, as do numerous indications in our own times. For man will always yearn to know, at least in an obscure way, what is the meaning of his life, of his activity, of his death. The very presence of the church recalls these problems to his mind. But only God, who created man to his own image and ransomed him from sin, provides the most adequate answer to these questions, and this he does through what he has revealed in Christ his Son, who became man. Whoever follows after Christ, the perfect man, becomes himself more of a man. For by his incarnation the Father's Word assumed, and sanctified through his cross and resurrection, the whole of man, body and soul, and through that totality the whole of nature created by God for man's use.

The Dignity of Human Nature

Thanks to this belief, the church can anchor the dignity of human nature against all tides of opinion, for example those which undervalue the human body or idolize it. By no human law can the personal dignity and liberty of man be so aptly safeguarded as by the gospel of Christ which has been entrusted to the church. For this gospel announces and proclaims the freedom of the sons of God, and repudiates all the bondage which ultimately results from sin (cf. Romans 8:14-17); it has a sacred reverence for the dignity of conscience and its freedom of choice, constantly advises that all human talents be employed in God's service and men's, and, finally, commends all to the charity of all (cf. Matthew 22:39).

This agrees with the basic law of the Christian dispensation. For though the same God is Savior and Creator, Lord of human history as well as of salvation history, in the divine arrangement itself, the rightful autonomy of the creature, and particularly of man is not withdrawn, but is rather re-established in its own dignity and strengthened in it.

The church, therefore, by virtue of the gospel committed to her, proclaims the rights of man; she acknowledges and greatly esteems the dynamic movements of today by which these rights are everywhere fostered. Yet these movements must be penetrated by the spirit of the gospel and protected against any kind of false autonomy. For we are tempted to think that our personal rights are fully ensured only when we are exempt from every requirement of divine law. But this way lies not the maintenance of the dignity of the human person, but its annihilation. ∾

UNITY AMONG CHRISTIANS

Pope John's efforts to further unity among Christians paved the way for the council's Unitatis Redintegratio, *(Decree on Ecumenism), in which the Catholic Church clearly expressed its deep regard for Christians of all denominations and its desire for the healing of divisions, for reconciliation, and for restoration. Excerpts are taken from paragraphs 1, 3-4, and 7-8.*

The restoration of unity among all Christians is one of the principal concerns of the Second Vatican Council. Christ the Lord founded one church and one church only. However, many Christian communions present themselves to men as the true inheritors of Jesus Christ; all indeed profess to be followers of the Lord but differ in mind and go their different ways, as if Christ himself were divided (cf. 1 Corinthians 1:13). Such division openly contradicts the will of Christ, scandalizes the world and damages the holy cause of preaching the gospel to every creature.

But the Lord of ages wisely and patiently follows out the plan of grace on our behalf, sinners that we are. In recent times more than ever before, he has been rousing divided Christians to remorse over their divisions and to a longing for unity. Everywhere large numbers have felt the impulse of this grace, and among our separated brethren also there increases from day to day the movement, fostered by the grace of the Holy Spirit, for the restoration of unity among all Christians. This movement toward unity is called "ecumenical." Those belong to it who invoke the Triune God and confess Jesus as Lord and Savior, doing this not merely as individuals but also as corporate bodies. For almost everyone regards the body in which he has heard the gospel as his church and indeed, God's church. All, however, though in different ways, long for the one visible church of God, a church truly universal and sent forth into the world that the world may be converted to the gospel and so be saved, to the glory of God.

The sacred council gladly notes all this. It has already declared its teaching on the church, and now, moved by a desire for the restoration of unity among all the followers of Christ, it wishes to set before all Catholics the ways and means by which they too can respond to this grace and to this divine call. . . .

Overcoming Obstacles

Even in the beginnings of this one and only church of God, there arose certain rifts (cf. 1 Corinthians 11:18-19; Galatians 1:6-9; 1 John 2:18-19) which the Apostle strongly condemned (cf. 1 Corinthians 1:11ff., 11:22). But in subsequent centuries much more serious dissensions made their appearance, and quite large communities came to be separated from full communion with the Catholic Church—for which, often enough, men of both sides were to blame. The children who are born into these communities and who grow up believing in Christ cannot be accused of the sin involved in the separation, and the Catholic Church embraces them as brothers, with respect and affection. For men who believe in Christ and have been truly baptized are in communion with the Catholic Church even though this communion is imperfect. The differences that exist in varying degrees between them and the Catholic Church—whether in doctrine and sometimes in discipline, or concerning the structure of the church—do indeed create many obstacles, sometimes serious ones, to full ecclesiastical communion. The ecumenical movement is striving to overcome these obstacles. But even in spite of them it remains true that all who have been justified by faith in baptism are members of Christ's body (Council of Florence, 1439, *Decree Exultate Deo*), and have a right to be called Christian, and so are correctly accepted as brothers by the children of the Catholic Church (cf. St. Augustine, *In Ps. 32*).

Moreover, some and even very many of the significant elements and endowments which together go to build up and give life to the church itself, can exist outside the visible boundaries of the Catholic Church: the written Word of God; the life of grace; faith, hope and charity, with the other interior gifts of the Holy Spirit; and visible elements too. All of these, which come from Christ and lead back to Christ, belong by right to the one church of Christ.

The brethren divided from us also use many liturgical actions of the Christian religion. These most certainly can truly engender a life of grace in ways that vary according to the condition of each church or community. These liturgical actions must be regarded as capable of giving access to the community of salvation.

It follows that the separated churches and communities as such, though we believe them to be deficient in some respects, have been by no means deprived of significance and importance in the mystery of salvation. For the Spirit of Christ has not refrained from using them as means of salvation which derive their efficacy from the very fullness of grace and truth entrusted to the church. . . .

The Work of Ecumenism

Today, in many parts of the world, under the inspiring grace of the Holy Spirit, many efforts are being made in prayer, word and action to attain that fullness of unity which Jesus Christ desires. The sacred council exhorts all the Catholic faithful to recognize the signs of the times and to take an active and intelligent part in the work of ecumenism.

The term "ecumenical movement" indicates the initiatives and activities planned and undertaken, according to the various needs of the church and as opportunities offer, to promote Christian unity. These are: first, every effort to avoid expressions, judgments, and actions which do not represent the condition of our separated brethren with truth and fairness and so make mutual relations with them more difficult; then, "dialogue" between competent experts from different churches and communities. At these meetings, which are organ-ized in a religious spirit, each explains the teaching of his communion in greater depth and brings out clearly its distinctive features. In such dialogue, everyone gains a truer knowledge and more just appreciation of the teaching and religious life of both communions. In addition, the way is prepared for cooperation between them in the duties for the common good of humanity which are demanded by every Christian conscience; and, wherever this is allowed, there is prayer in common. Finally, all are led to examine their own faithfulness to Christ's will for the church and accordingly to undertake with vigor the task of renewal and reform.

When such actions are undertaken prudently and patiently by the Catholic faithful, with the attentive guidance of their bishops, they promote justice and truth, concord and collaboration, as well as the spirit of brotherly love and unity. This is the way that, when the obstacles to perfect ecclesiastical communion have been gradually overcome, all Christians will at last, in a common celebration of the Eucharist, be gathered into the one and only church in that unity which Christ bestowed on his church from the beginning. We believe that this unity subsists in the Catholic Church as something she can never lose, and we hope that it will continue to increase until the end of time. . . .

A Change of Heart

There can be no ecumenism worthy of the name without a change of heart. For it is from renewal of the inner life of our minds (cf. Ephesians 4:24), from self-denial and an unstinted love, that desires of unity take their rise and develop in a mature way. We should therefore pray to the Holy Spirit for the grace to be genuinely self-denying, humble, gentle in the service of others, and to have an attitude of brotherly generosity toward them. St. Paul says: "I, therefore, a prisoner for the Lord, beg you to lead a life worthy of the calling to which you have been called, with all humility and meekness, with patience, forbearing one another in love, eager to maintain the unity of the Spirit in the bond of peace" (Ephesians 4:1-3). This exhortation is directed especially to those raised to sacred Orders precisely that the work of Christ may be continued. He came among us "not to be served but to serve" (Matthew 20:28).

The words of St. John hold good about sins against unity: "If we say we have not sinned, we make him a liar, and his word is not in us" (1 John 1:10). So we humbly beg pardon of God and of our separated brethren, just as we forgive them that trespass against us.

All the faithful should remember that the more effort

they make to live holier lives according to the gospel, the better will they further Christian unity and put it into practice. For the closer their union with the Father, the Word and the Spirit, the more deeply and easily will they be able to grow in mutual brotherly love.

"Spiritual Ecumenism"

This change of heart and holiness of life, along with public and private prayer for the unity of Christians, should be regarded as the soul of the whole ecumenical movement and merits the name, "spiritual ecumenism."

It is a recognized custom for Catholics to have frequent recourse to that prayer for the unity of the church which the Savior himself on the eve of his death so fervently appealed to his Father: "That they may all be one" (John 17:21).

In certain special circumstances, such as the prescribed prayers "for unity" and during ecumenical gatherings, it is allowable, indeed desirable that Catholics should join in prayer with their separated brethren. Such prayers in common are certainly an effective means of obtaining the grace of unity, and they are a true expression of the ties which still bind Catholics to their separated brethren. "For where two or three are gathered together in my name, there am I in the midst of them" (Matthew 18:20). ❧

THE CALL TO THE LAITY

The great breath of new life that Pope John wanted to see infused into the church culminated in a fervent call by the council Fathers to the laity to take its mission into the world. One of the great gifts of Vatican II has been the response of the laity to this call. A key document of the council, Lumen Gentium *(Dogmatic Constitution on the Church), outlined the role of the laity in the world. Excerpts are taken from paragraphs 31 and 33-38).*

The term "laity" is here understood to mean all the faithful except those in holy Orders and those in the state of religious life specially approved by the church. These faithful are by baptism made one body with Christ and are constituted among the People of God; they are in their own way made sharers in the priestly, prophetical and kingly functions of Christ, and they carry out for their own part the mission of the whole Christian people in the church and in the world.

What specifically characterizes the laity is their secular nature. It is true that those in holy Orders can at times be engaged in secular activities, and even have a secular profession. But they are by reason of their particular vocation especially and professedly ordained to the sacred ministry. Similarly, by their state in life, religious give splendid and striking testimony that the world cannot be transformed and offered to God without the spirit of the beatitudes. But the laity, by their very vocation, seek the kingdom of God by engaging in temporal affairs and by ordering them according to the plan of God. They live in the world, that is, in each and in all of the secular professions and occupations. They live in the ordinary circumstances of family and social life, from which the very web of their existence is woven. They are called there by God that by exercising their proper function and led by the spirit of the gospel, they may work for the sanctification of the world from within as a leaven. In this way they may make Christ known to others, especially by the testimony of a life resplendent in faith, hope and charity. Therefore, since they are tightly bound up in all types of temporal affairs it is their special task to order and to throw light upon these affairs in such a way that they may come into being and then continually increase according to Christ to the praise of the Creator and the Redeemer. . . .

Energizing the Church

The laity are gathered together in the People of God and make up the body of Christ under one head. Whoever they are, they are called upon, as living members, to expend all their energy for the growth of the church and its continuous sanctification, since this very energy is a gift of the Creator and a blessing of the Redeemer.

The lay apostolate, however, is a participation in the salvific mission of the church itself. Through their baptism and confirmation all are commissioned to that apostolate by the Lord himself. Moreover, by the sacraments, especially the Holy Eucharist, that charity toward God and man which is the soul of the apostolate is communicated and nourished. Now the laity are called in a special way to make the church present and operative in those places and circumstances where only through them can it become the salt of the earth (see encyclical of Pius XI, *Quadragesimo anno*, May 15, 1931). Thus every layman, in virtue of the very gifts bestowed upon him, is at the same time a witness and a living instrument of the mission of the church itself, "according to the measure of Christ's bestowal" (Ephesians 4:7).

Besides this apostolate, which certainly pertains to all Christians, the laity can also be called in various ways to a more direct form of cooperation in the apostolate of the hierarchy. This was the way certain men and women assisted Paul the apostle in the gospel, laboring much in the Lord (cf. Philippians 4:3; Romans 16:3ff.). Further, they have the capacity to assume from the hierarchy certain ecclesiastical functions, which are to be performed for a spiritual purpose.

Upon all the laity, therefore, rests the noble duty of working to extend the divine plan of salvation to all men of each epoch and in every land. Consequently, may every opportunity be given them so that, according to their abilities and the needs of the times, they may zealously participate in the saving work of the church.

Living in the Spirit

The supreme and eternal priest, Christ Jesus, since he wills to continue his witness and service also through the laity, vivifies them in this Spirit and increasingly urges them on to every good and perfect work.

For besides intimately linking them to his life and his mission, he also gives them a sharing in his priestly function of offering spiritual worship for the glory of God and the salvation of men. For this reason, the laity, dedicated to Christ and anointed by the Holy Spirit, are marvelously called and wonderfully prepared so that ever more abundant fruits of the Spirit may be produced in them. For all their works, prayers and apostolic endeavors, their ordinary married and family life, their daily occupations, their physical and mental relaxation, if carried out in the Spirit, and even the hardships of life, if patiently borne—all these become "spiritual sacrifices acceptable to God through Jesus Christ" (1 Peter 2:5). Together with the offering of the Lord's body, they are most fittingly offered in the celebration of the Eucharist. Thus, as those everywhere who adore in holy activity, the laity consecrate the world itself to God. . . .

Just as the sacraments of the New Law, by which the life and the apostolate of the faithful are nourished, prefigure a new heaven and a new earth (cf. Revelations 21:1), so too the laity go forth as powerful proclaimers of a faith in things to be hoped for (cf. Hebrews 11:1), when they courageously join to their profession of faith a life springing from faith. This evangelization, that is, this announcing of Christ by a living testimony as well as by the spoken word, takes on a specific quality and a special force in that it is carried out in the ordinary surroundings of the world.

In connection with the prophetic function, that state of life which is sanctified by a special sacrament is obviously of great importance, namely, married and family life. For where Christianity pervades the entire mode of family life, and gradually transforms it, one will find there both the practice and an excellent school of the lay apostolate. In such a home husbands and wives find their proper vocation in being witnesses of the faith and love of Christ to one another and to their children. The Christian family loudly proclaims both the present virtues of the kingdom of God and the hope of a blessed life to come. Thus by its example and its witness it accuses the world of sin and enlightens those who seek the truth.

Evangelizing the World

Consequently, even when preoccupied with temporal cares, the laity can and must perform a work of great value for the evangelization of the world. For even if some of them have to fulfill their religious duties on their own, when there are no sacred ministers or in times of persecution, and even if many of them devote all their energies to apostolic work, still it remains for each one of them to cooperate in the external spread and the dynamic growth of the kingdom of Christ in the world. Therefore, let the laity devotedly strive to acquire a more profound grasp of revealed truth, and let them insistently beg of God the gift of wisdom.

Christ, becoming obedient even unto death and because of this exalted by the Father (cf. Philippians 2:8-9), entered into the glory of his kingdom. To him all things are made subject until he subjects himself and all created things to the Father that God may be all in all (cf. 1 Corinthians 15:27-28). Now Christ has communicated this royal power to his disciples that they might be constituted in royal freedom and that by true penance and a holy life they might conquer the reign of sin in themselves (cf. Romans 6:12). Further, he has shared this power so that serving Christ in their fellow men they might by humility and patience lead their brethren to that King for whom to serve is to reign. But the Lord wishes to spread his kingdom also by means of the laity, namely, a kingdom of truth and life, a kingdom of holiness and grace, a kingdom of justice, love, and peace. In this kingdom creation itself will be delivered from its slavery to corruption into the freedom of the glory of the sons of God (cf. Romans 8:21). Clearly then a great promise and a great trust is committed to the disciples: "All things are yours, and you are Christ's, and Christ is God's" (1 Corinthians 3:23).

The faithful, therefore, must learn the deepest meaning and the value of all creation, as well as its role in the harmonious praise of God. They must assist each other to live holier lives even in their daily occupations. In this way the world may be permeated by the spirit of Christ and it may more effectively fulfill its purpose in justice, charity and peace. The laity have the principal role in the overall fulfillment of this duty. Therefore, by their competence in secular training and by their activity, elevated from within by the grace of Christ, let them vigorously contribute their effort, so that created goods may be perfected by human labor, technical skill and civic culture for the benefit of all men according to the design of the Creator and the light of his Word. May the goods of this world be more equitably distributed among all men, and may they in their own way be conducive to universal progress in human and Christian freedom. In this manner, through the members of the church, will Christ progressively illumine the whole of human society with his saving light.

Transforming the Culture

Moreover, let the laity also by their combined efforts remedy the customs and conditions of the world, if they are an inducement to sin, so that they all may be conformed to the norms of justice and may favor the practice of virtue rather than hinder it. By so doing they will imbue culture and human activity with genuine moral values; they will better prepare the field of the world for the seed of the Word of God, and at the same time they will open wider the doors of the church by which the message of peace may enter the world. . . .

A great many wonderful things are to be hoped for from this familiar dialogue between the laity and their spiritual leaders: in the laity a strengthened sense of personal responsibility, a renewed enthusiasm, a more ready application of their talents to the projects of their spiritual leaders. The latter, on the other hand, aided by the experience of the laity, can more clearly and more incisively come to decisions regarding both spiritual and temporal matters. In this way, the whole church, strengthened by each one of its members, may more effectively fulfill its mission for the life of the world.

Each individual layman must stand before the world as a witness to the resurrection and life of the Lord Jesus and a symbol of the living God. All the laity as a community and each one according to his ability must nourish the world with spiritual fruits (cf. Galatians 5:22). They must diffuse in the world that spirit which animates the poor, the meek, the peace makers—whom the Lord in the gospel proclaimed as blessed (cf. Matthew 5:3-9). In a word, "Christians must be to the world what the soul is to the body" (*Epistle ad Diognetum*, 6). ❧

Sources and Acknowledgments

All selections in chapter two, "My Soul Is in These Pages," reprinted from *Journal of a Soul* by Pope John XXIII, translated by Dorothy White. Copyright © 1980 by Geoffrey Chapman, a division of Cassell Ltd. Used by permission of Doubleday, a division of Random House, Inc.

All selections in chapter three, "To My Beloved Family," reprinted from *Letters to His Family* by Pope John XXIII, translated by Dorothy White. English translation copyright © 1969 by Geoffrey Chapman, a division of Cassell Ltd. Published in the U.S. by McGraw-Hill Book Company, New York.

Selections on pages 57, 61, 63, 69, 80, 84, and 94 reprinted from *Days of Devotion* by Pope John XXIII, translated by Dorothy White. Copyright © 1967 by The K. S. Giniger Co., Inc. Used by permission of Viking Penguin, a division of Penguin Putnam Inc.

Selection on page 58 reprinted from *Mission to France, 1944-1953*, by Angelo Giuseppe Roncalli, translated by Dorothy White. English translation copyright © by Geoffrey Chapman, a division of Cassell Ltd. Published in the U.S. by McGraw-Hill Book Company, New York.

The following selections, reprinted from the encyclicals of Pope John XXIII, are available on the web at www.vatican.va and are used by permission of the Vatican:

Excerpts on pages 62, 64, 78, and 87 from *Ad Petri Cathedram*, Encyclical of Pope John XXIII on Truth, Unity and Peace, issued on June 29, 1959.

Excerpts on pages 74, 81, 85, and 93 from *Pacem in Terris*, Encyclical of Pope John XXIII on Establishing Universal Peace in Truth, Justice, Charity and Liberty, issued on April 11, 1963.

Excerpt on page 91 from *Mater et Magistra*, Encyclical of Pope John XXIII on Christianity and Social Progress, issued May 15, 1961.

Excerpt on page 99 from *Paenitentiam Agere*, Encyclical of Pope John XXIII on the Need for the Practice of Interior and Exterior Penance, issued on July 1, 1962.

Selection on page 101 reprinted from Pope John XXIII's Opening Speech to the Second Vatican Council, available on the web at Christus Rex Inc. (www.christusrex.org).

Other Resources from The Word Among Us Press

Also available from the Wisdom Series:
Welcoming the New Millennium, Wisdom from Pope John Paul II
   A collection of some of the Holy Father's most inspiring writings, on subjects ranging from prayer and forgiveness to evangelism and marriage.

Live Jesus! Wisdom from Saints Francis de Sales and Jane de Chantal
   Gentle, sensible and loving advice from two saints who knew how to recognize opportunities in their daily lives to put their love for God into action.

Walking with the Father, Wisdom from Brother Lawrence
   Learn from this seventeenth-century Carmelite brother how to abide in God's presence no matter what you are doing or how busy you are.

Touching the Risen Christ, Wisdom from the Fathers
   The writings from the early Church Fathers become more accessible to the contemporary reader in this collection of sermons in an easy-to-read translation.

From the Gospel Devotional Commentary Series:
Matthew: A Devotional Commentary
Mark: A Devotional Commentary
Luke: A Devotional Commentary
John: A Devotional Commentary
Leo Zanchettin, General Editor

   Enjoy reading and praying through the gospels with commentaries that include each passage of scripture with a faith-filled meditation.

Books on the Saints:
A Great Cloud of Witnesses: The Stories of 16 Saints and Christian Heroes by Leo Zanchettin and Patricia Mitchell

I Have Called You by Name: The Stories of 16 Saints and Christian Heroes by Patricia Mitchell

   Each book contains inspiring biographies, along with selections of the saints' own writings.

To order call 1-800-775-9673
www.wau.org